MUSIC 2000

Volume

Student Workbook

Classroom Theory Lessons for Secondary Students

By DONALD MOORE

Project Manager: Brian Busch
Cover Design: Debbie Lipton

TABLE OF CONTENTS VOLUME II PAGE

37. THE GRAND STAFF AND MIDDLE C

The **GRAND STAFF** allows a performer to read music on the TREBLE and BASS CLEF STAVES* at the same time.

***CURVED BRACKET** and BAR LINE*

The **CURVED BRACKET** is used for music read by KEYBOARDISTS.

***STRAIGHT BRACKET** and BAR LINE*

The **STRAIGHT BRACKET** is used for music read by SINGERS and INSTRUMENTALISTS.

* Staves – Plural of staff

DIRECTIONS: ❶ Draw two CURVED BRACKETS to form GRAND STAVES on the left and two STRAIGHT BRACKETS to form GRAND STAVES on the right. ❷ Include the BAR LINES and CLEF SIGNS.

Example

Example

THE GRAND STAFF COMPLETE

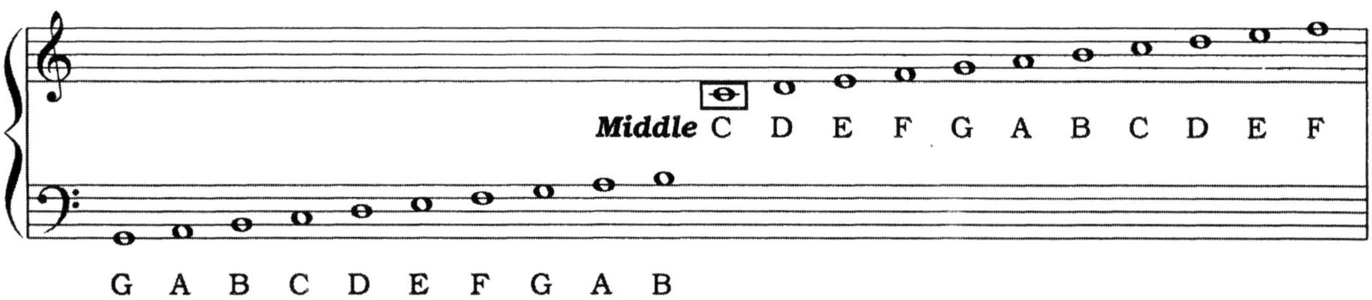

TWO WAYS OF DRAWING MIDDLE C

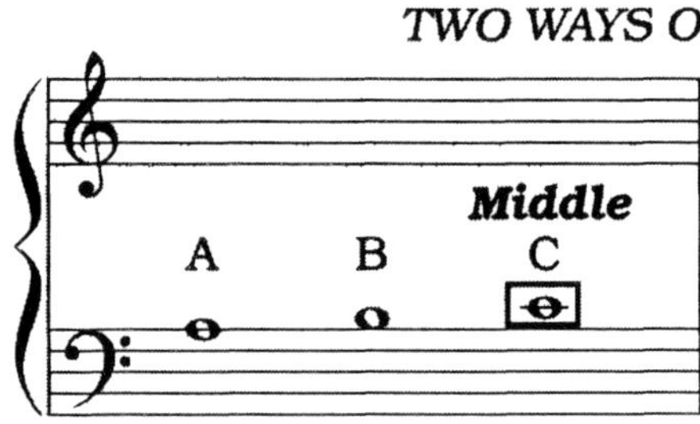

From the BASS CLEF STAFF

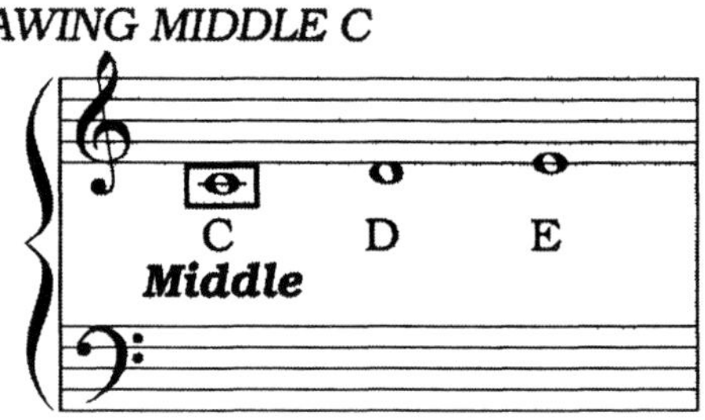

From the TREBLE CLEF STAFF

DIRECTIONS: Circle the MIDDLE Cs.

POP THAT CORN

Vivace *McDonald*

SING OUT WITH JOY

Allegro *Moore*

38. STEPS, LEAPS AND INTERVALS

STEPS

A NOTE (PITCH) in a SPACE moving up or down to a different NOTE (PITCH) on the next nearest LINE is called a **STEP**.

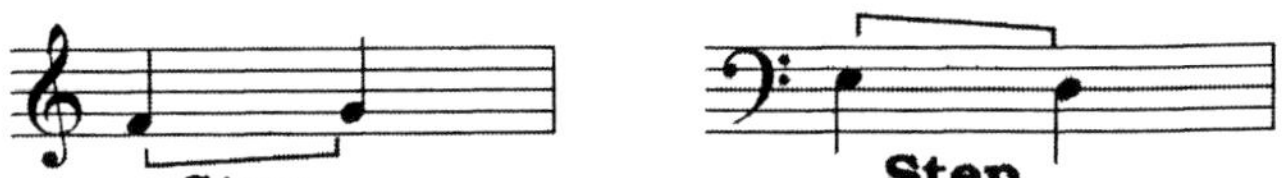

Step **Step**
From a SPACE to the next nearest LINE

A NOTE (PITCH) on a LINE moving up or down to a different NOTE (PITCH) in the next nearest SPACE is *also* called a **STEP**.

Step **Step**
From a LINE to the next nearest SPACE

DIRECTIONS: Write an **S** (STEP) between NOTES that move by STEP.

ALL THROUGH THE NIGHT *Welsh*

Example

LEAPS

Any NOTE moving to another NOTE that does not move by **STEP** is call a **LEAP**. ***At least one NOTE is always LEAPED.***

Leap

A (B,C,D) E

NOTES LEAPED

Leap

D (C) B

NOTE LEAPED

DIRECTIONS: Write an **L** (LEAP) between NOTES that move by LEAP and an **S** between NOTES that move by STEP.

BIG BASKETS *Moore*

Example

An **INTERVAL** is the DISTANCE from one NOTE to another NOTE.
***INTERVALS** can be **HARMONIC** or **MELODIC**.*

***HARMONIC INTERVALS** (Vertical)*
are performed at the same time.

***MELODIC INTERVALS** (Horizontal)*
are performed separately.

DIRECTIONS: Write an **H** for a HARMONIC INTERVAL or **M** for a MELODIC INTERVAL.

INTERVAL *type* **M** ...... **H** ....
Example

39. THE INTERVAL OF A PRIME AND SECOND AND THE SCORE

The NAME of an INTERVAL is determined by the number of LINES and SPACES used.

PRIME INTERVALS

A **PRIME INTERVAL** moves from one NOTE to another NOTE of the same PITCH.

HARMONIC SECONDS

MELODIC SECONDS

An **INTERVAL** of a **SECOND** involves the distance of *ONE* LINE + *ONE* SPACE.

The NOTES of a ***HARMONIC SECOND*** *must be placed next to each other to avoid overlapping.*

The lowest NOTE is always on the left of the stem.

DIRECTIONS: Write **1** for a PRIME INTERVAL or **2** for an INTERVAL of a SECOND.

INTERVAL number: 2 ...... (*Example*) ....

A **SCORE** includes all the music needed to perform a composition.

Pianists, organists, conductors and other musicians read several STAVES of a* ***SCORE*** *at once.*

A ***CLOSED SCORE*** shows all the music on two STAVES.

An ***OPEN SCORE*** shows the VOCAL or INSTRUMENTAL PARTS on separate STAVES.

*Plural for STAFF

DIRECTIONS: Answer the following questions about the *STAR-SPANGLED BANNER* shown below in CLOSED and OPEN SCORE.

1. How many STAVES does the CLOSED SCORE have? ______________________
2. How many STAVES does the OPEN SCORE have? ______________________
3. In the OPEN SCORE, there are ten MELODIC INTERVALS of a SECOND. One of them is already circled. Circle the other nine. ***Some of the SECONDS overlap each other.***

(CLOSED SCORE)

THE STAR-SPANGLED BANNER

Smith

*S=SOPRANO A=ALTO T=TENOR B=BASS

(OPEN SCORE)

THE STAR-SPANGLED BANNER

Smith

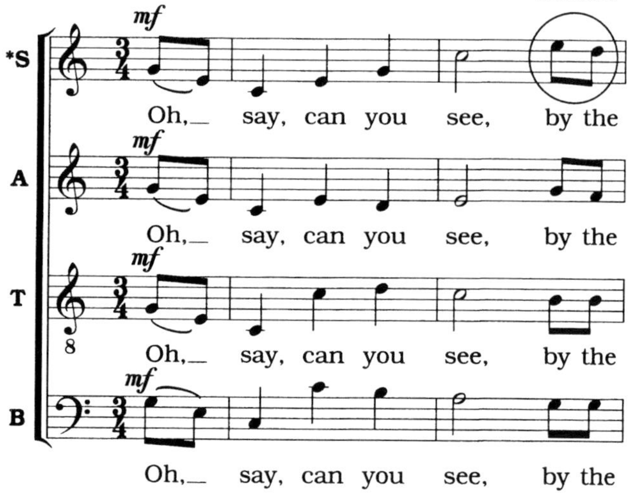

40. SCORE READING

Musicians read the GRAND STAFF VERTICALLY (up and down) as they perform the music HORIZONTALLY (left to right). Study how each BEAT is aligned VERTICALLY.

CHORALE

Lento *Harmonized by Bach*

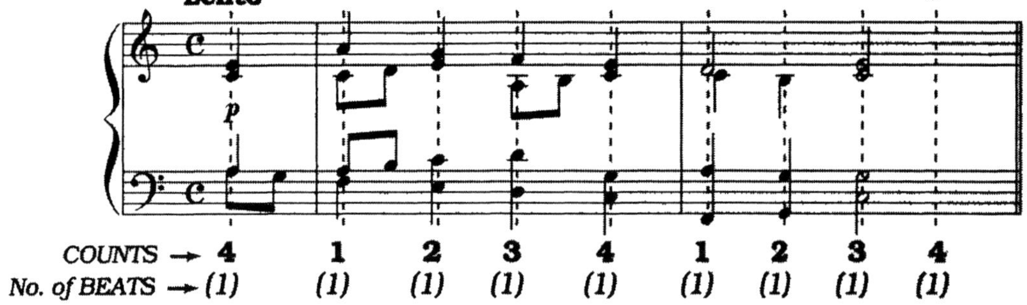

DIRECTIONS: ❶ Draw a STRAIGHT VERTICAL LINE through each STAFF for each BEAT (1,2,3,etc.) in the following SCORES. ***Be precise.*** ❷ Write the COUNTING on the dotted lines. ***Do not divide the BEATS.***

AMERICA, THE BEAUTIFUL

Moderately *Ward*

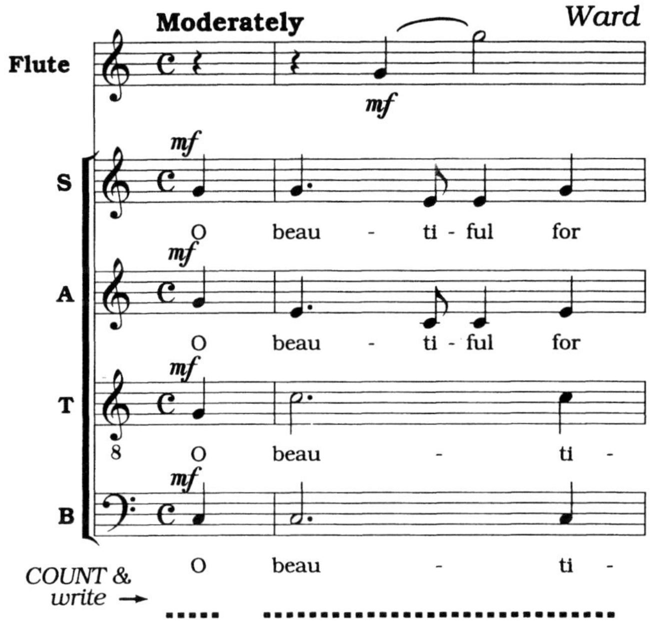

PEDAL POINT

Largo *Moore*

DIRECTIONS: There are eight (8) INTERVALS of a SECOND in *AMERICA*, including the two NOTES already circled. Circle each INTERVAL of a SECOND. ***Some of the SECONDS overlap each other.***

AMERICA

Allegretto *Carey*

REVIEW OF LESSONS 37-40

DIRECTIONS: Circle TRUE or FALSE for each statement.

TRUE FALSE 1. An interval is the distance from one note to another note.

TRUE FALSE 2. This  is an harmonic interval.

TRUE FALSE 3. This 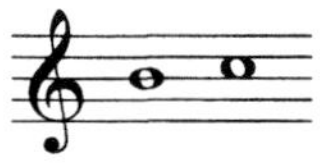 is a melodic interval.

TRUE FALSE 4. This  is a prime interval.

TRUE FALSE 5. The size of an interval is determined by the clef sign.

TRUE FALSE 6. Score is another name for common time.

TRUE FALSE 7. A closed score displays all the music on two staves.

TRUE FALSE 8. An open score displays one voice or instrumental part per staff.

DIRECTIONS: There are eight (8) middle Cs in *FROLIC*. Circle the middle Cs.

FROLIC

Presto *Moore*

DIRECTIONS: ❶ There are thirteen (13) melodic intervals of a second in the score below. Circle each interval of a second. ❷ Also draw a straight vertical line through each staff for each beat. ***Be precise.*** ❸ Write the counting on the dotted line. ***Do not divide the beats.***

YANKEE DOODLE

Presto *U.S.*

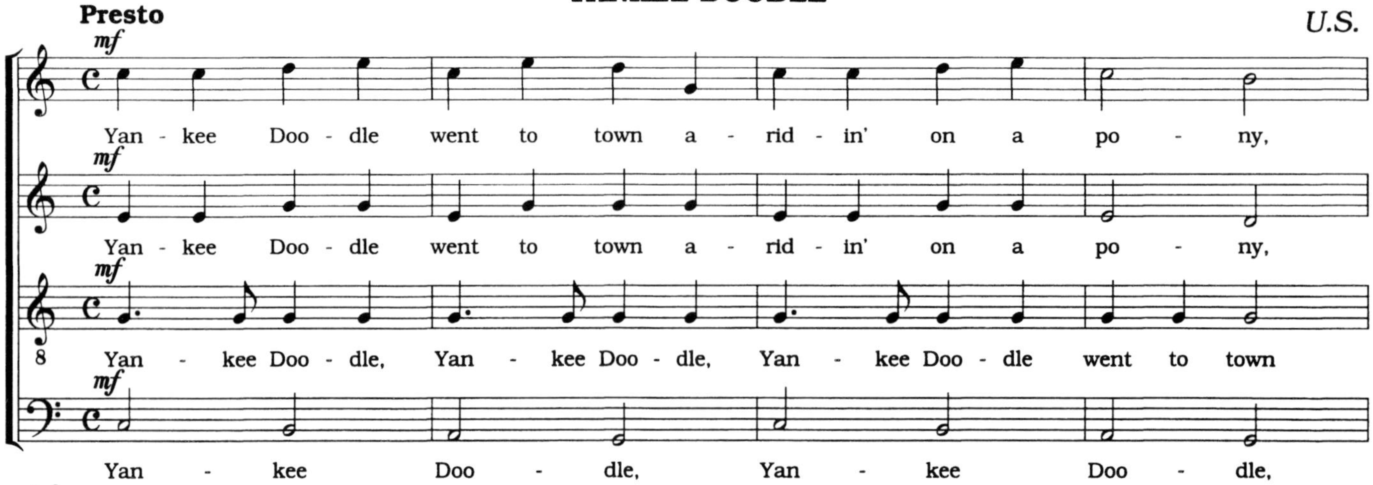

Count & write →

41. THE INTERVAL OF A THIRD AND STEM DIRECTION

THE INTERVAL OF A THIRD

HARMONIC THIRDS

MELODIC THIRDS

An ***INTERVAL of a THIRD*** *involves the distance of THREE (3) LINES and SPACES.*

DIRECTIONS: Indentify PRIME INTERVALS with a number **1**, SECONDS with a **2** and THIRDS with a **3**.

INTERVAL number → **3** ....

Example

RULE: When two or more NOTES are stacked or connected by a BEAM, the NOTE farthest from the middle LINE determines the STEM DIRECTION. NOTES that are equal distance from the middle LINE have STEMS DOWN.

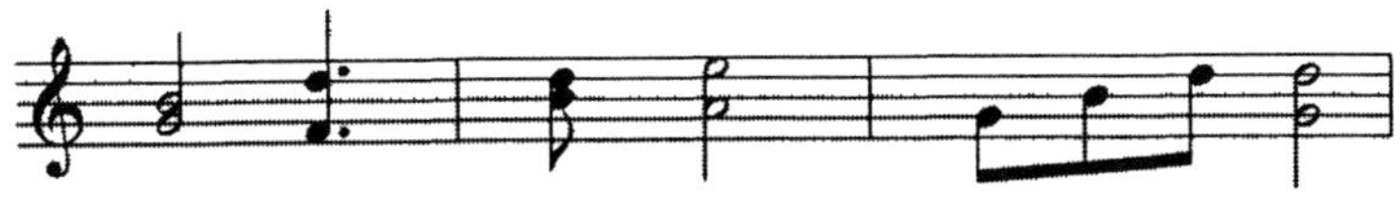

STEMS Up *STEMS Down* *STEMS Down (Equal Distance)*

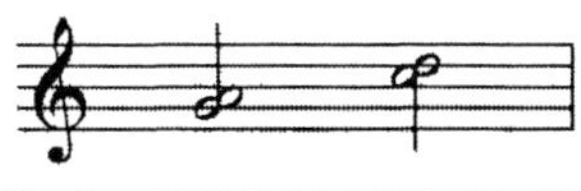

STEMS for HARMONICS SECONDS are placed in the middle. The lower NOTE is always placed to the left of the STEM.

DIRECTIONS: Add a STEM to each HARMONIC INTERVAL.

Added STEM

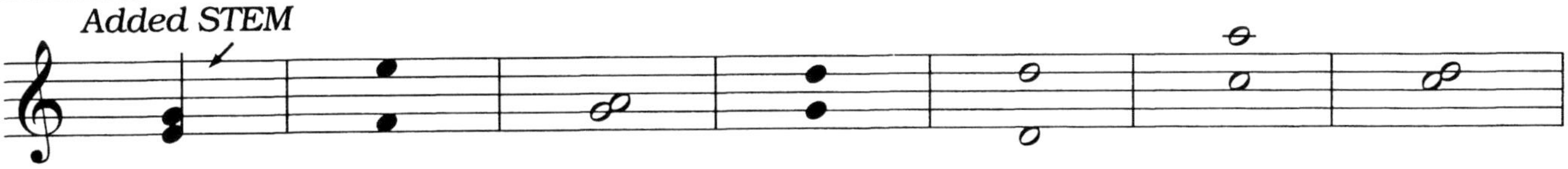

Example

DIRECTIONS: ❶ Add a similar NOTE *above* the given NOTE to make a HARMONIC INTERVAL of a THIRD.
❷ Add a stem to each INTERVAL.

Given NOTE

Example

DIRECTIONS: Write the number of each MELODIC INTERVAL on the dotted line.

Lightly **SPRING HAS SPRUNG** *DePaul*

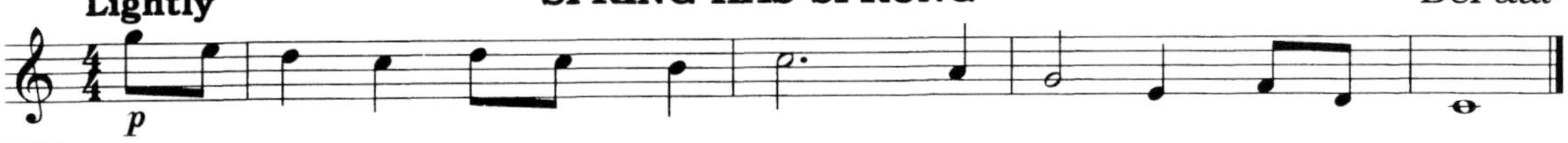

MELODIC INTERVAL number → **3** **2** ....

Example

42. THE SYSTEM

A **SYSTEM** consists of several STAVES joined together.
*Several **SYSTEMS** usually appear on a page of music.*

To locate a particular NOTE on a page of music, musicians refer to the:

❶ **SYSTEM NUMBER** ❷ **MEASURE NUMBER** ❸ **BEAT NUMBER** ❹ **PART***

The circled NOTE is in the:

1. First **SYSTEM**
2. Second full MEASURE
3. Third BEAT
4. Flute **PART**

The boxed NOTE is in the:

1. Second **SYSTEM**
2. Second MEASURE
3. First BEAT
4. Piano, left hand **PART** *(BASS CLEF)*

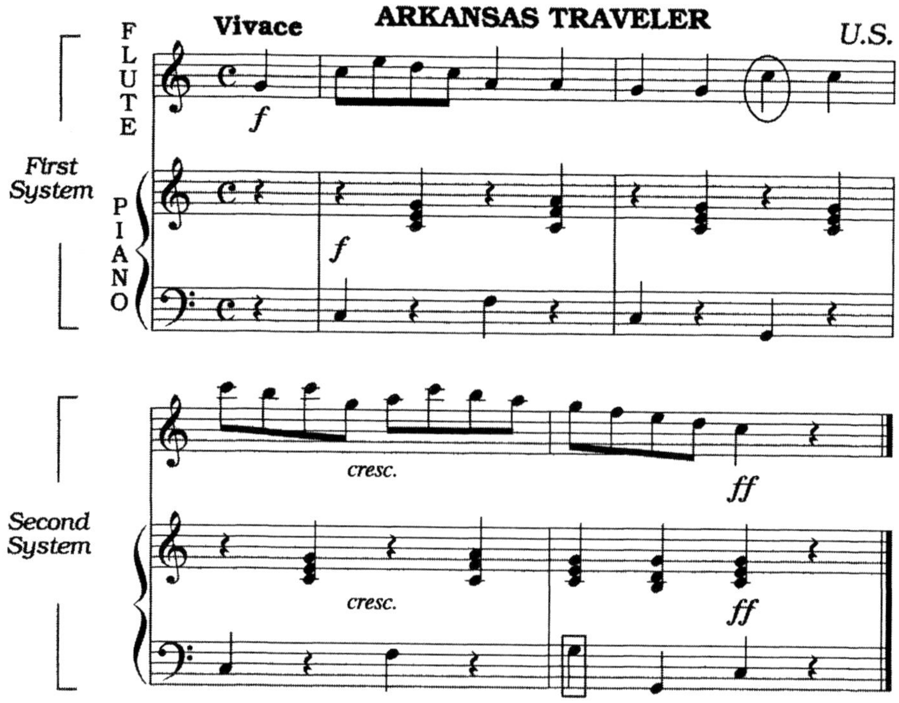

* The music of a particular voice or instrument

DIRECTIONS: Write the number of each TREBLE *(piano, right hand)* MELODIC INTERVAL and each BASS *(piano, left hand)* MELODIC INTERVAL on the dotted lines.

DIRECTIONS: Fill in the blanks.

The circled NOTE is in/on the:

1. ____________________ SYSTEM
2. ____________________ MEASURE
3. ____________________ BEAT
4. ____________________ PART

go on to next system

The boxed NOTE is in/on the:

1. ____________________ SYSTEM
2. ____________________ MEASURE
3. ____________________ BEAT
4. ____________________ PART

43. THE INTERVAL OF A FOURTH

THE INTERVAL OF A FOURTH

HARMONIC FOURTHS

MELODIC FOURTHS

An ***INTERVAL of a FOURTH*** *involves the distance of FOUR (4) LINES and SPACES.*

DIRECTIONS: Write the number of each INTERVAL.

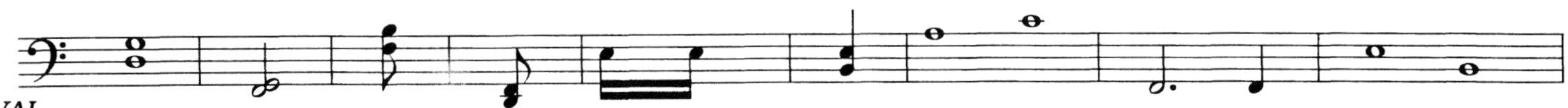

INTERVAL number → 4 (*Example*)

DIRECTIONS: ❶ Add a similar NOTE *below* the given NOTE to make a HARMONIC INTERVAL of a FOURTH.
❷ Add a STEM to each INTERVAL.

Given NOTE

Example

DIRECTIONS: Write the number of each MELODIC INTERVAL.

Smoothly

ON A SNOWY EVENING

Dakins

INTERVAL number → 4 (*Example*)

DIRECTIONS: Write the LETTER NAMES of the NOTES to form words.

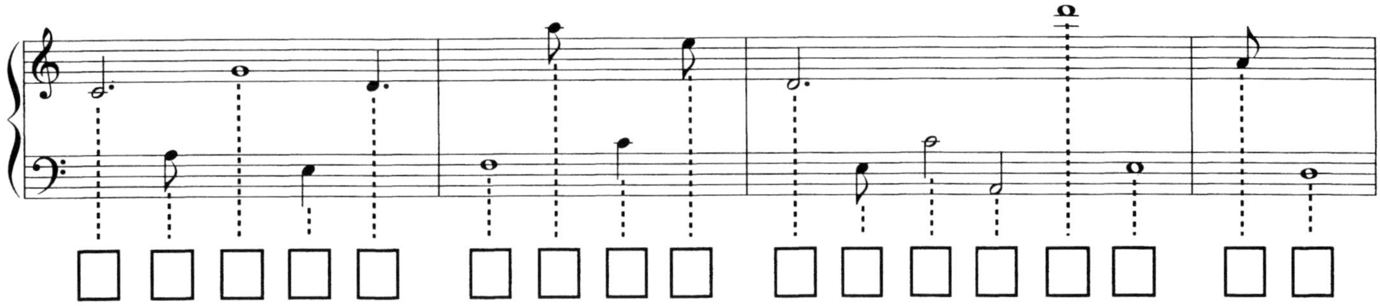

44. HARMONY AND THE ALTO AND SOPRANO PARTS

HARMONY is several NOTES of different PITCHES performed at once.

UNISON
(No HARMONY)

Two PART HARMONY

Three PART HARMONY

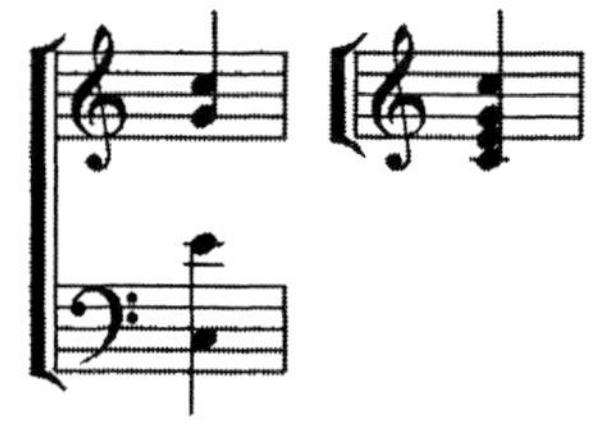

Four PART HARMONY

DIRECTIONS: Write the number of HARMONY PARTS (2, 3 or 4) in each MEASURE. *If there is no HARMONY, write U for UNISON (UNIS.).*

....

VOICE PARTS written on the TREBLE CLEF STAFF are called the **SOPRANO** (higher NOTE) and the **ALTO** (lower NOTE).

DIRECTIONS: Circle each ALTO NOTE.

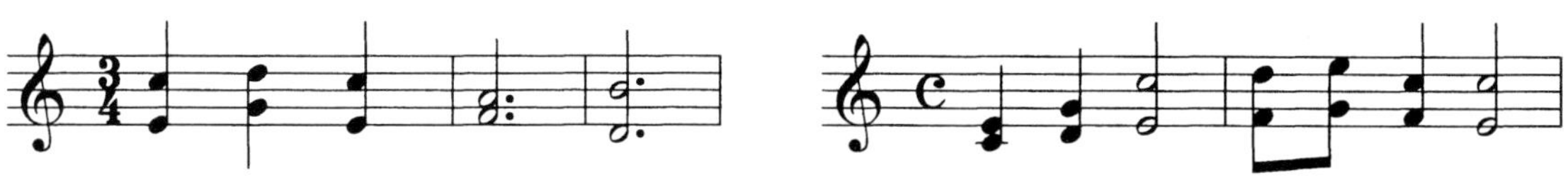

TYPICAL VOICE RANGES FOR ALTO AND SOPRANO PARTS

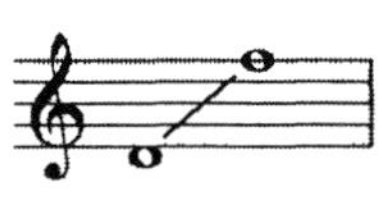

SOPRANO RANGE

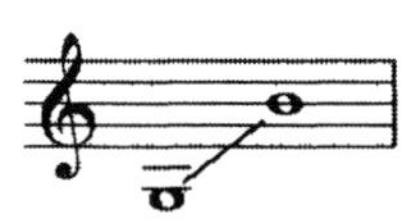

ALTO RANGE

DIRECTIONS: Study each NOTE below and decide whether the SOPRANO or ALTO PART should perform the NOTE. ***Some notes could be performed by either the SOPRANO or ALTO.*** Write **S** for SOPRANO, **A** for ALTO or **E** for EITHER.

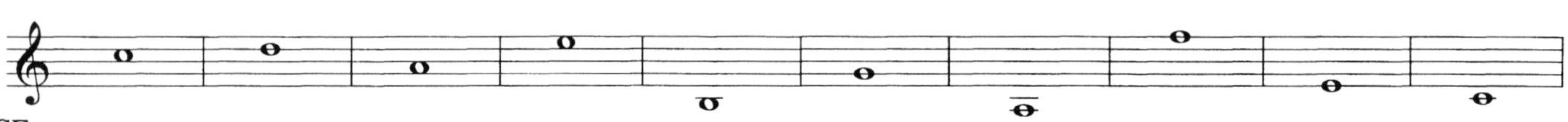

VOICE PART → S ....
Example

REVIEW OF LESSONS 41-44

DIRECTIONS: Write the harmonic interval number for each soprano-alto part.

BILLY BOY

Allegro *English*

DIRECTIONS: ❶ Draw a straight vertical line through each system for each beat of *RONDO.* ❷ Write the counting for each measure. *Do not divide the beats.*

DIRECTIONS:

Answer the following questions:

1. How many systems are in *RONDO?* __________

2. The circled note is in/on the:
   - ________ System
   - ________ Measure
   - ________ Beat
   - ________ Part

2. The boxed note is in/on the:
   - ________ System
   - ________ Measure
   - ________ Beat
   - ________ Part

Moderato **RONDO** *Mozart*

DIRECTIONS: Study each example below and then decide whether the alto or soprano part would be the best choice to perform the note. Write **S** for soprano or **A** for alto.

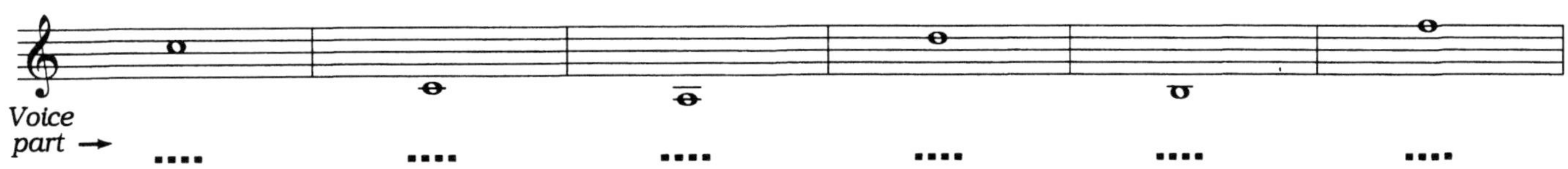

45. THE INTERVAL OF A FIFTH AND THE TENOR AND BASS PARTS

THE INTERVAL OF A FIFTH

HARMONIC FIFTHS

MELODIC FIFTHS

*An **INTERVAL of a FIFTH** involves the distance of FIVE (5) LINES and SPACES.*

DIRECTIONS: Write the number of each INTERVAL.

INTERVAL number → ....

DIRECTIONS: ❶ Add a similar NOTE above the given NOTE to make a HARMONIC FIFTH. ❷ Add a STEM to each INTERVAL.

Given NOTE

Example

VOICE PARTS written on the BASS CLEF STAFF are called the **TENOR** (higher NOTE) and the **BASS** (lower NOTE).

In OPEN SCORE, the **TENOR PART is written on the TREBLE CLEF STAFF.*

DIRECTIONS: Draw a circle around each TENOR NOTE.

TYPICAL VOICE RANGES FOR TENOR AND BASS PARTS

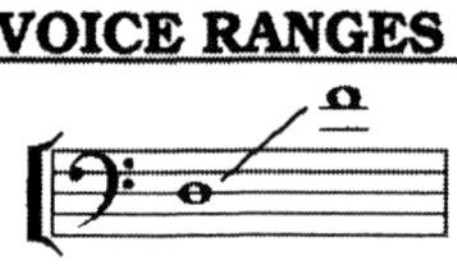

TENOR RANGE

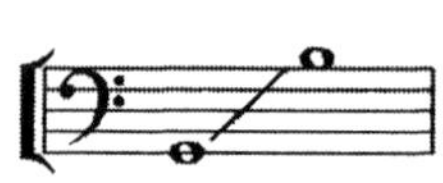

BASS RANGE

DIRECTIONS: Study each NOTE below and decide whether the TENOR or BASS PART should perform the NOTE. ***Some NOTES could be performed by either the TENOR or BASS.*** Write **T** for TENOR PART, **B** for BASS PART or **E** for EITHER PART.

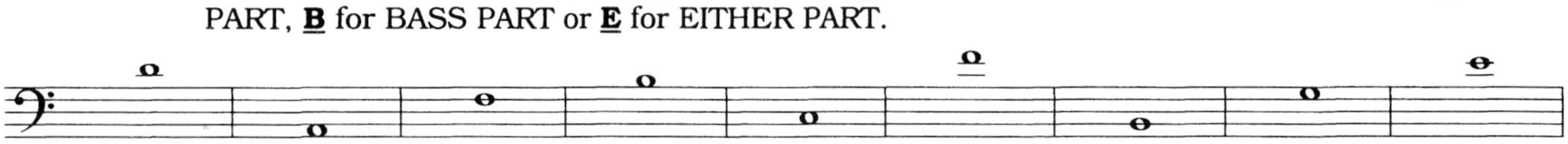

VOICE PART → ....

46. VOICE AND HARMONY IDENTIFICATION

TYPICAL VOICE PART RANGES

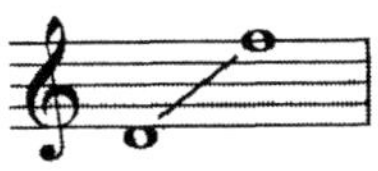

SOPRANO RANGE

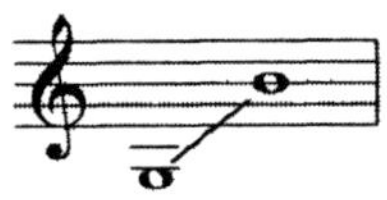

ALTO RANGE

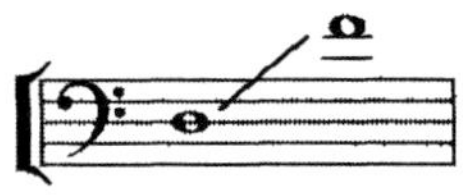

TENOR RANGE

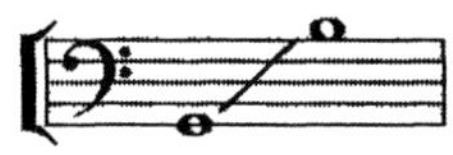

BASS RANGE

DIRECTIONS: Write the VOICE PART that would be *best* for each MELODY.

❶ LOCH LOMOND *Scottish*

VOICE PART ______________________

❷ ALL THROUGH THE NIGHT *Welsh*

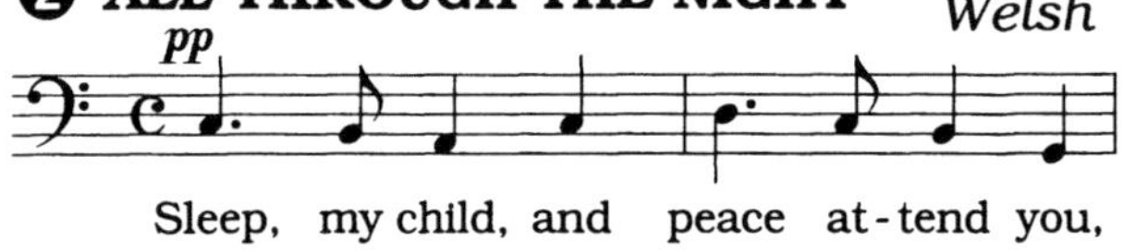

VOICE PART ______________________

❸ I LOVE NOODLES *Moore*

VOICE PART ______________________

❹ ERIE CANAL *American*

VOICE PART ______________________

❺ WAYFARING STRANGER *American*

VOICE PART ______________________

This is **FOUR PART HARMONY.**
(CLOSED SCORE)

**In OPEN SCORE, the TENOR PART is written on the TREBLE CLEF STAFF.*

DIRECTIONS: Identify the VOICE PARTS for the following HARMONY. ***A single NOTE written in the BASS CLEF should be considered the BASS PART.***

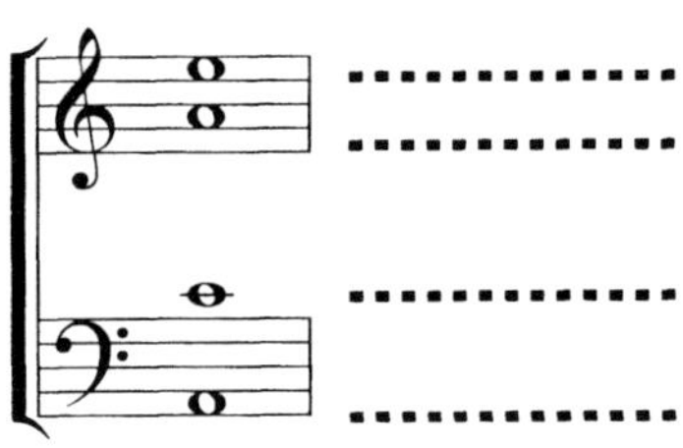

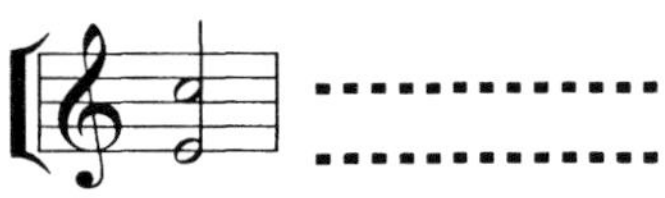

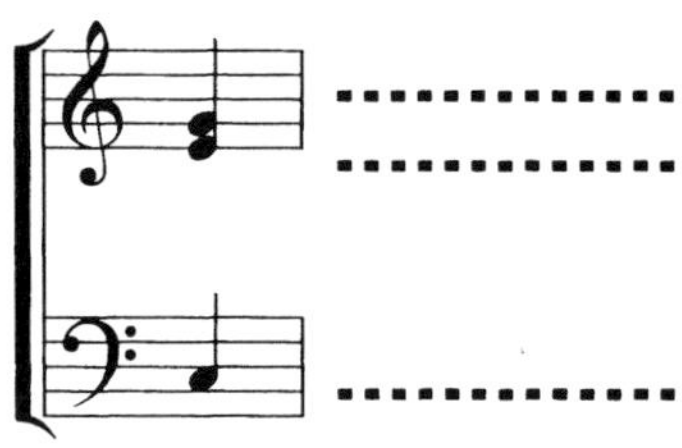

47. THE INTERVAL OF A SIXTH

THE INTERVAL OF A SIXTH

HARMONIC SIXTHS

MELODIC SIXTHS

*An **INTERVAL of a SIXTH** involves the distance of SIX (6) LINES and SPACES.*

DIRECTIONS: Write the number of each INTERVAL.

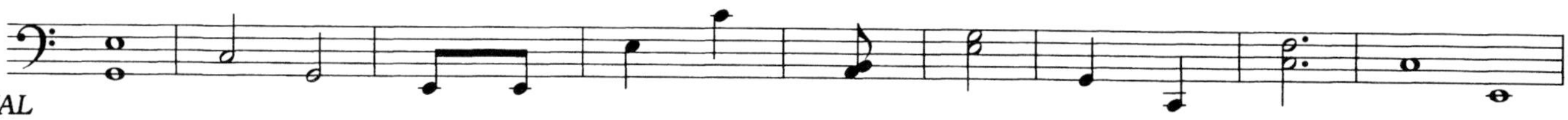

INTERVAL number → ....

DIRECTIONS: ❶ Add a similar NOTE below the given NOTE to make a HARMONIC SIXTH. ❷ Add a STEM to each INTERVAL.

Given NOTE

Example

DIRECTIONS: There are five (5) HARMONIC INTERVALS of a SIXTH in *OH, WHAT GLORY.* Circle each SIXTH.

How many VOICE PARTS are in *OH, WHAT GLORY?* ______

The circled NOTE is in the:

__________ SYSTEM

__________ MEASURE

__________ BEAT

__________ PART

Allegro **OH, WHAT GLORY** *Spiritual*

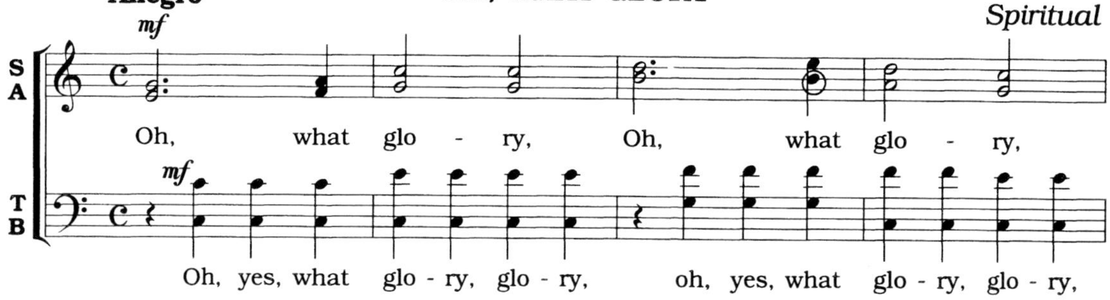

The boxed NOTE is in the:

__________ SYSTEM

__________ MEASURE

__________ BEAT

__________ PART

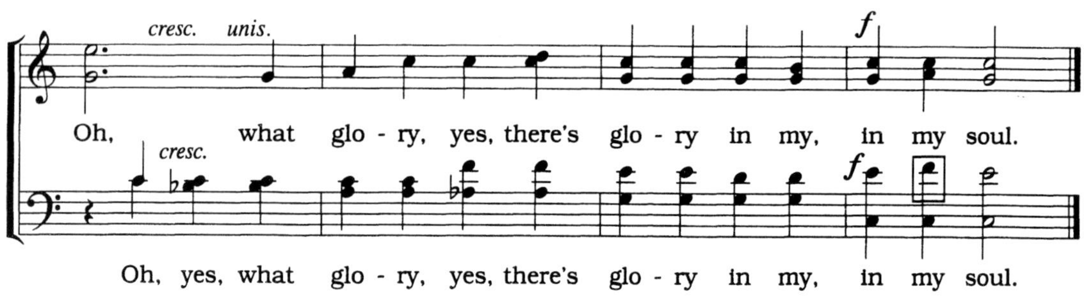

48. COUNTERPOINT

COUNTERPOINT* is two or more independent MELODIES performed at the same time.

The independent MELODIES must differ: RHYTHMICALLY and/or MELODICALLY, but should compliment each other HARMONICALLY.

OLD MacDONALD *U.S.*

*Also known as POLYPHONY

DIRECTIONS: Circle the title of each music composition that is an example of COUNTERPOINT.

MINUET

Moderato *Moore*

JOY TO THE WORLD

Allegretto *Handel*

THE LONE PRAIRIE

Slowly *American*

DIRECTIONS: Write the HARMONIC INTERVAL number below each TENOR-BASS PART.

Fast **HORN FIFTH** *Donaldson*

HARMONIC INTERVAL number → 6 ....

Example

REVIEW OF LESSONS 45-48

DIRECTIONS: Match each term on the left with the best example on the right.

_____ Interval of a fifth
_____ Tenor voice range
_____ Interval of a third
_____ Counterpoint
_____ Alto voice range
_____ Three part harmony
_____ Interval of a second
_____ Interval of a sixth
_____ Soprano voice range
_____ Interval of a fourth
_____ Tenor part
_____ Soprano part
_____ Melodic intervals
_____ Bass part
_____ Prime interval
_____ System
_____ Harmonic intervals
_____ Alto part
_____ Bass voice range
_____ Four part harmony

DIRECTIONS: Answer the following questions.

1. Is *THE YELLOW ROSE* an example of counterpoint?

   YES *NO*

2. The circled note is in the:
   ___________ SYSTEM
   ___________ MEASURE
   ___________ BEAT
   ___________ PART

3. The boxed note is in the:
   ___________ SYSTEM
   ___________ MEASURE
   ___________ BEAT
   ___________ PART

THE YELLOW ROSE OF TEXAS

49. INTERVAL OF A SEVENTH AND VOICE PART READING

THE INTERVAL OF A SEVENTH

HARMONIC SEVENTHS

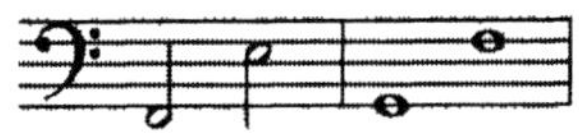

MELODIC SEVENTHS

*An **INTERVAL of a SEVENTH** involves the distance of SEVEN (7) LINES and SPACES.*

DIRECTIONS: Write the number of each INTERVAL.

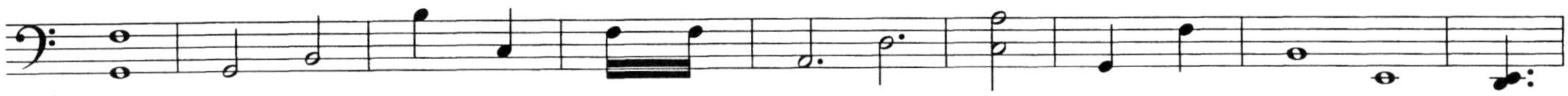

INTERVAL number → ....

DIRECTIONS: ❶ Add a similar NOTE *above* the given NOTE to make a HARMONIC SEVENTH. ❷ Add a STEM to each INTERVAL.

Given NOTE

Example

TWO-PART COUNTERPOINT WRITTEN ON ONE STAFF

*Example 1 show **TWO-PART COUNTERPOINT** written on two STAVES (OPEN SCORE).*
*Example 2 shows the same **TWO-PART COUNTERPOINT** written on one STAFF (CLOSED SCORE).*

Example 1 *(OPEN SCORE)* **VALLEY SONG** *U.S.*

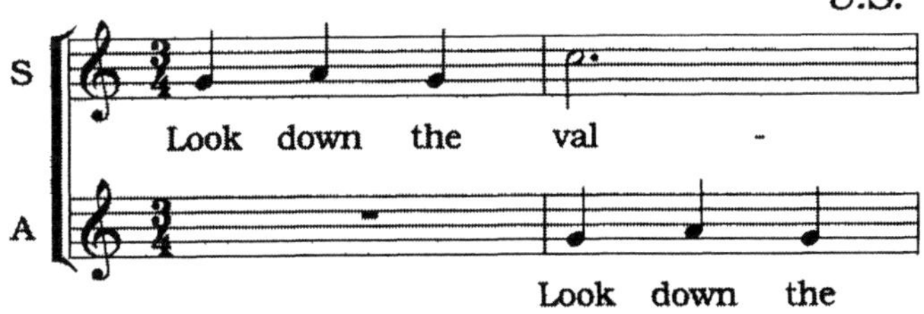

Example 2 *(CLOSED SCORE)* **VALLEY SONG** *U.S.*

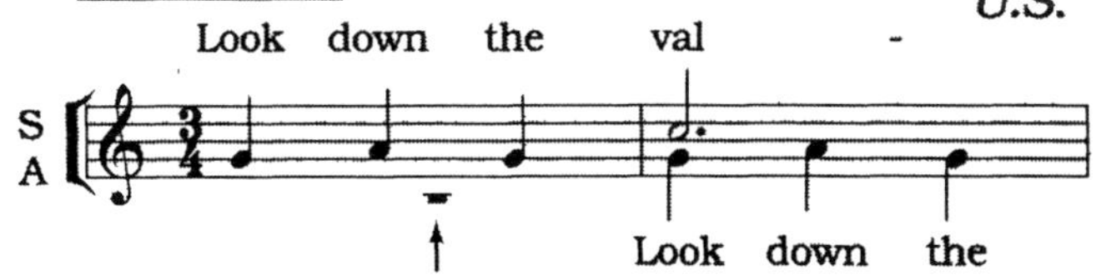

(ALTO REST)

In CLOSED SCORE, SOPRANOS and TENORS read VOICE PARTS **(TWO-PART COUNTERPOINT)** with STEMS UP. ALTOS and BASSES read VOICE PARTS with STEMS DOWN.

DIRECTIONS: Below are examples of TWO-PART COUNTERPOINT written on one STAFF. Circle the BASS and ALTO STEMS DOWN PARTS, including any RESTS.

SYLLABLE SONG

Moore

O COME, ALL YE FAITHFUL

Wade

50. IMITATION

IMITATION is one VOICE PART echoing or repeating another VOICE PART.

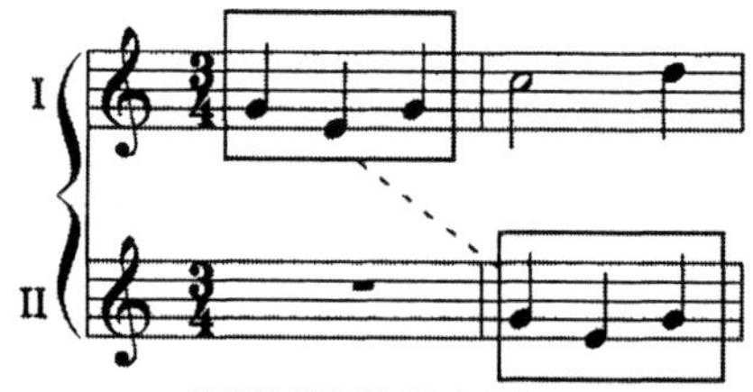

STRICT IMITATION

VOICE PART II is a ***STRICT*** *(EXACT)* ***IMITATION*** *of VOICE PART I*

FREE IMITATION

VOICE PART II is not a ***STRICT*** ***IMITATION*** *of VOICE PART I*

DIRECTIONS: Circle the title of the examples that use IMITATION (STRICT or FREE).

INVENTION IN C MAJOR

Bach

TOM TURKEY

Donaldson

HYMN

Palestrina

DIRECTIONS: ❶ Complete the following example of TWO PART COUNTERPOINT by writing a STRICT IMITATION of PART I. ❷ Align the BEATS of both PARTS and add the words.

ARE YOU SLEEPING?

French

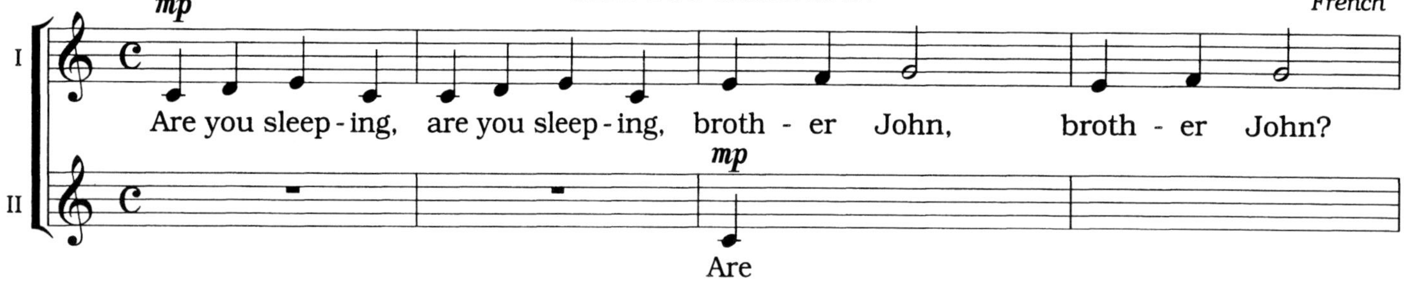

DIRECTIONS: ❶ Write the MELODIC INTERVAL number between each STEMS UP TENOR NOTE. ❷ Do the same for each STEMS DOWN BASS NOTE.

DONA NOBIS PACEM

German

51. THE OCTAVE (INTERVAL OF AN EIGHTH)

THE OCTAVE (INTERVAL OF AN EIGHTH)

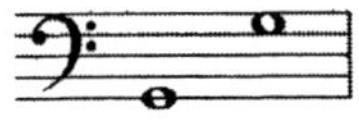

HARMONIC OCTAVE **MELODIC OCTAVE**

*An **OCTAVE** involves the distance of EIGHT (8) LINES and SPACES.*

DIRECTIONS: Write the number of each INTERVAL

INTERVAL number → ....

DIRECTIONS: ❶ Draw a similar NOTE below the given NOTE to make a HARMONIC OCTAVE.
❷ Add a STEM to each INTERVAL.

Given NOTE

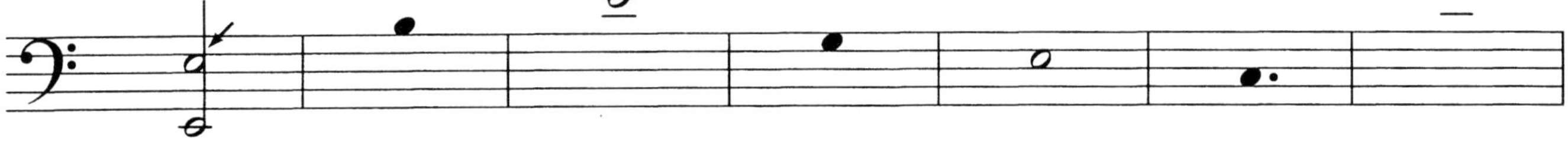

Example

DIRECTIONS: Study the SCORE of *AMEN* and answer the questions.

AMEN

Lutkin

1. Is AMEN an example of COUNTERPOINT? YES NO
2. How many VOICE PARTS does the SCORE have? ______________
3. Is IMITATION used in the SCORE? YES NO
4. Is the ALTO PART a FREE IMITATION of the TENOR PART? YES NO
5. Is the SOPRANO PART a STRICT IMITATION of the BASS PART? YES NO
6. What is the INTERVAL between the circled NOTES C and B? ______________
7. What is the INTERVAL between the boxed NOTES G and C? ______________
8. Draw a vertical line through the fourth BEAT of every MEASURE (both STAVES of the SYSTEM).

52. THE CANON

A **CANON** consists of a VOICE PART that is STRICTLY IMITATED by another VOICE PART.

SING A SONG

Moore

DIRECTIONS: Circle the title of the examples that are CANONS.

Allegretto **BAROQUE MELODY** *Hayes*

SONG OF GOOD CHEER

Moderato *English*

Allegro **BIG LADDERS** *Donaldson*

DIRECTIONS: ❶ Complete the following CANON by writing PART II in STRICT IMITATION of PART I.
❷ Include the words and align the BEATS of both PARTS.

Moderato **THE JOLLY MILLER** *Moorman*

DIRECTIONS: Write the HARMONIC INTERVAL number below each SOPRANO-ALTO VOICE PART.

Smoothly **LOVELY NIGHT** *Chwatal*

REVIEW OF LESSONS 49-52

SING WE NOW A MERRY SONG

Joyfully *Moore*

DIRECTIONS: Answer the following questions about *SING WE NOW A MERRY SONG.*

1. How many voice parts does the score have? ______________________
2. What voice parts strictly imitate the first measure of the soprano part? ______________
3. What voice part strictly imitates several measures of the soprano part? ______________
4. Circle the alto and bass voice parts. ***Include any rests.***

DIRECTIONS: ❶ Complete the canon below by writing a strict imitation of part II. ❷ Include the words and align the beats of both parts.

SING AND REJOICE

Moderately *Bradbury*

DIRECTIONS: Write on the dotted line the melodic interval numbers for the bass part.

GAVOTTE

Presto *Telemann*

53. THE HALF STEP AND ACCIDENTAL SIGNS

The PITCH of a NOTE can be raised or lowered a **HALF STEP**.
*A **HALF STEP** on the keyboard is from one key to the next nearest key regardless of color.*

White *to* Black   Black *to* White   White *to* White

These 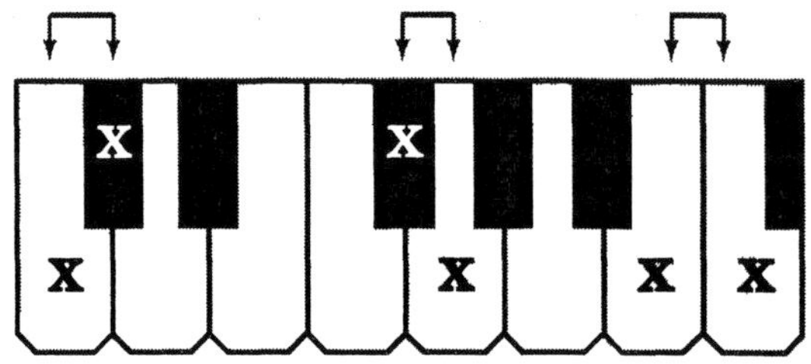 are HALF STEPS

DIRECTIONS: Circle the keyboards that display a HALF STEP.

1. 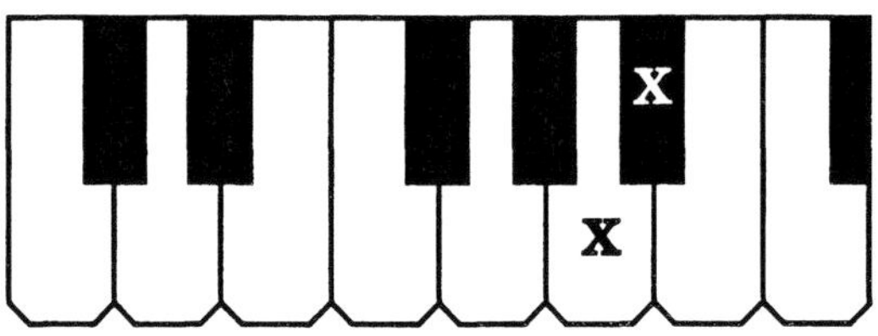

2. 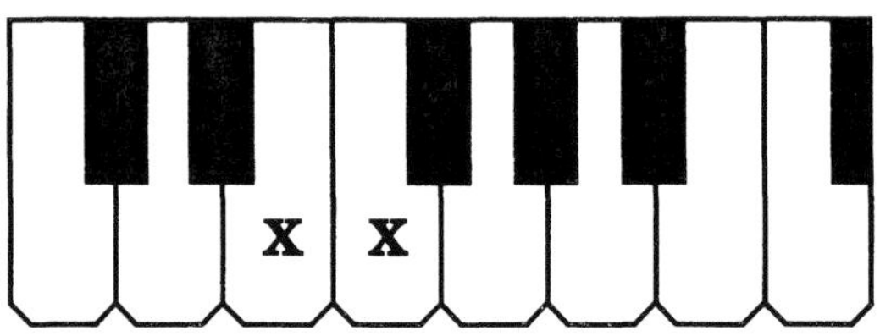

3. 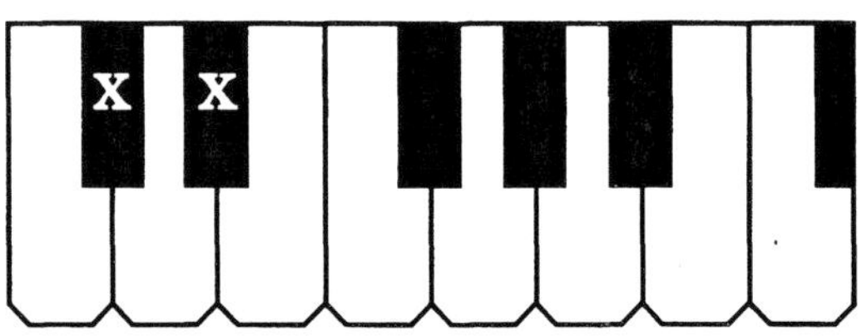

4. 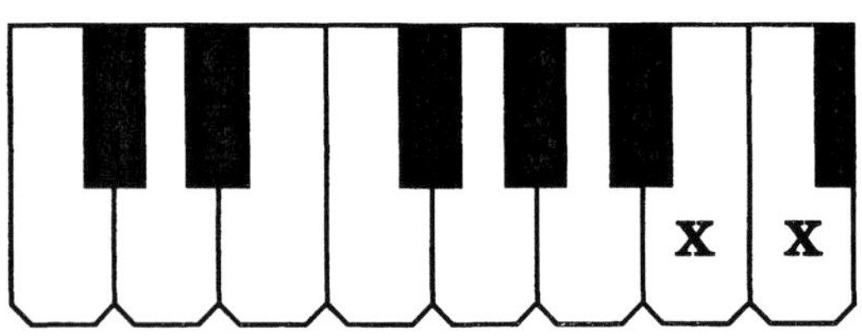

5. 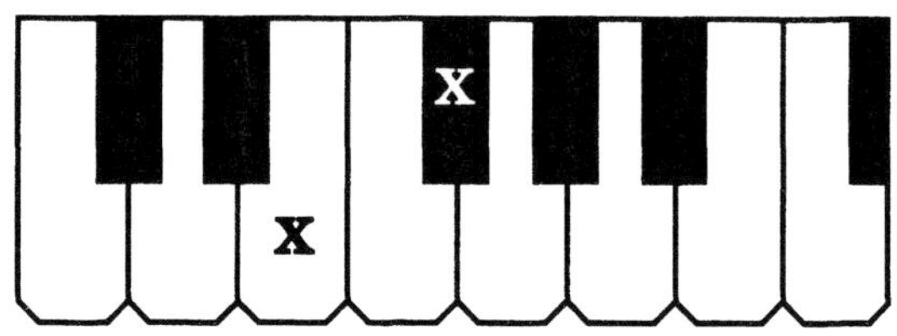

6. 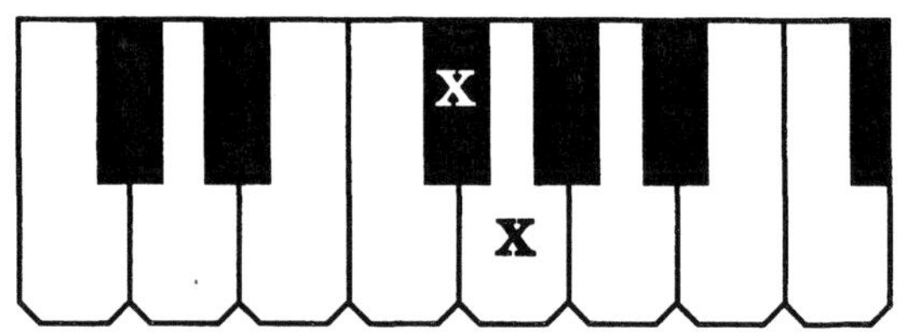

7. 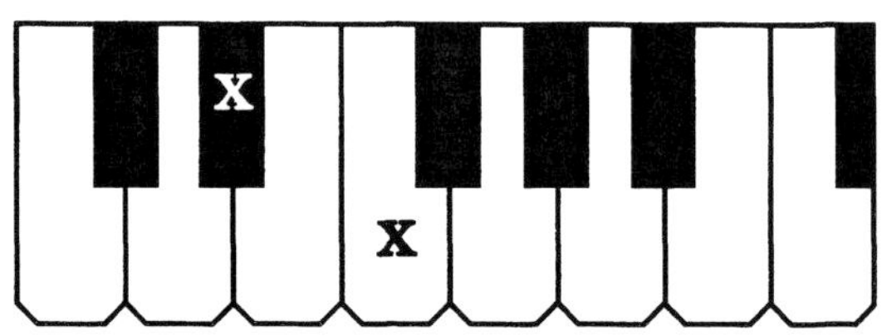

8. 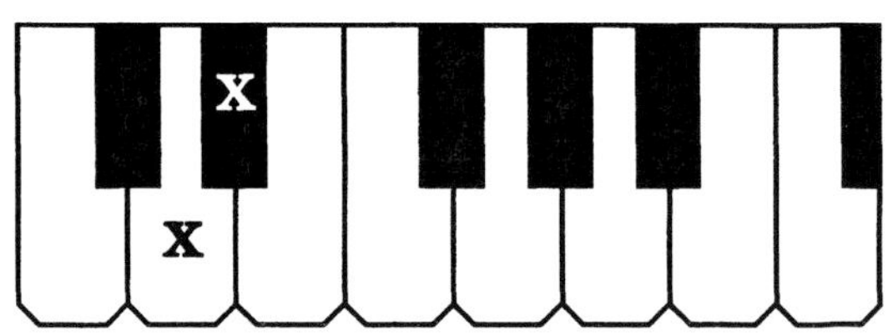

These ♭ ♯ ♮ are **ACCIDENTAL SIGNS.**

ACCIDENTAL SIGNS are used to raise or lower the PITCH of a NOTE one HALF STEP.

DIRECTIONS: Circle the ACCIDENTAL SIGNS

54. THE SHARP SIGN

This ♯ is a **SHARP SIGN**.

A SHARP SIGN raises the PITCH of a NOTE ONE (1/2) HALF STEP.

DIRECTIONS: Circle the SHARPED NOTES.

The **SHARP SIGN** is placed before the NOTE and must be on the same LINE or SPACE as the NOTE.

However, the SHARP SIGN is placed after the LETTER NAME. ⟶

DIRECTIONS: ❶ Draw a SHARP SIGN before each NOTE on the same LINE or SPACE. ❷ Write the LETTER NAME of each NOTE. *Include the SHARP SIGN.*

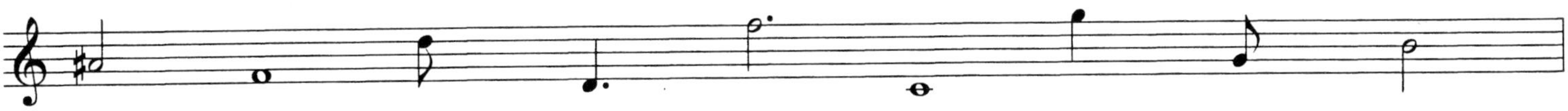

A♯ ....

Example

Below are **SHARPED NOTES** as they appear on the GRAND STAFF and keyboard.

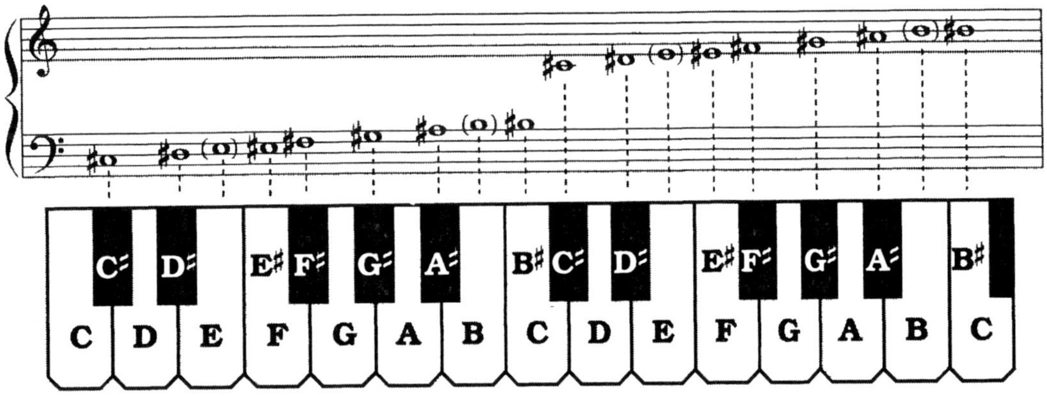

DIRECTIONS: Each keyboard displays a HALF STEP. The first NOTE of each HALF STEP is given on the STAFF below. Add the second NOTE of the HALF STEP, using a SHARP SIGN when necessary. ***Some examples have two possible answers.***

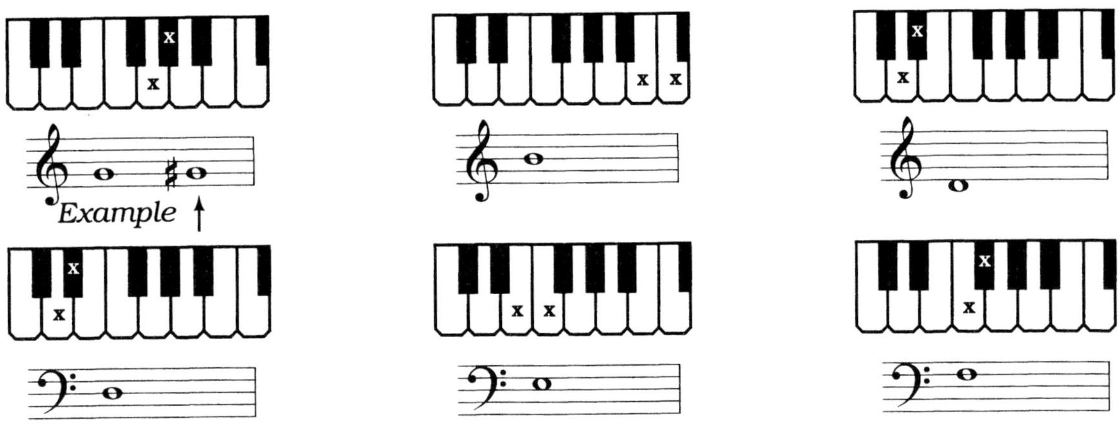

Example ↑

55. MORE SCORE READING

DIRECTIONS: ❶ Study the VOICE PARTS of *OLD MacDONALD.* Write the SOPRANO PART exactly as written on STAFF I and the ALTO PART exactly as written on STAFF II. ❷ Include the words with each VOICE PART.

OLD MacDONALD

Traditional

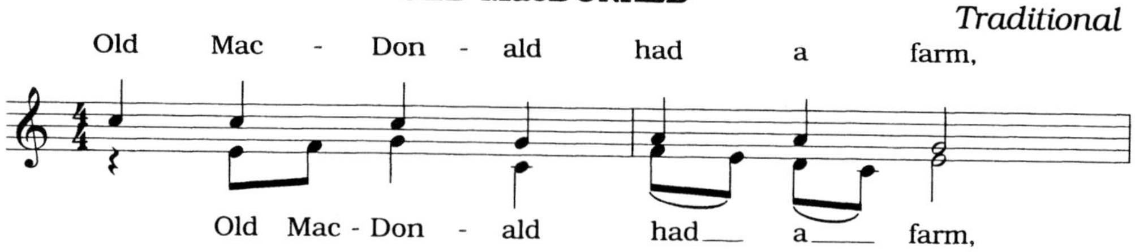

STAFF I *SOPRANO PART:* **S**

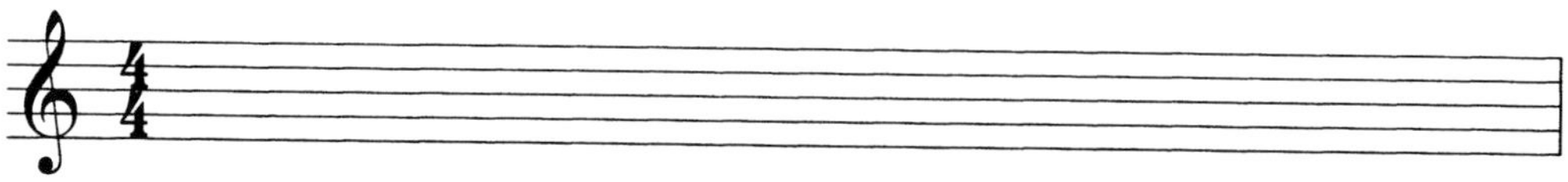

STAFF II *ALTO PART:* **A**

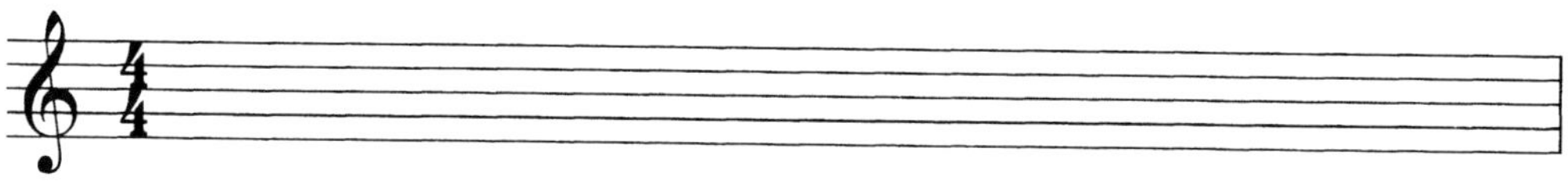

DIRECTIONS: Write the HARMONIC INTERVAL number of the TENOR-BASS PART on the dotted line.

GOOD KING WENCESLAS

England

T
B

HARMONIC INTERVAL number →

....

DIRECTIONS: ❶ Circle all the SHARPED NOTES. ❷ Write the name of the SHARPED NOTE including the SHARP SIGN above the STAFF.

MOONLIGHT BAY

With a lilt

Madden-Wenrich

REALLY SHARP

Moderato

Moore

56. THE FLAT SIGN

This ♭ is a **FLAT SIGN**.

*A **FLAT SIGN** lowers the PITCH of a NOTE ONE (½)HALF STEP.*

DIRECTIONS: Circle the FLATTED NOTES.

The **FLAT SIGN** is placed before the NOTE and must be on the same LINE or SPACE as the NOTE.

*However, the **FLAT SIGN** is placed after the LETTER NAME.* ⟶

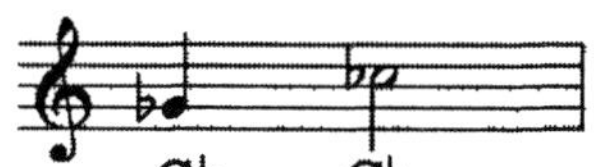

DIRECTIONS: ❶ Draw a FLAT SIGN before each NOTE on the same LINE or SPACE. ❷ Write the LETTER NAME of each NOTE. ***Include the FLAT SIGN.***

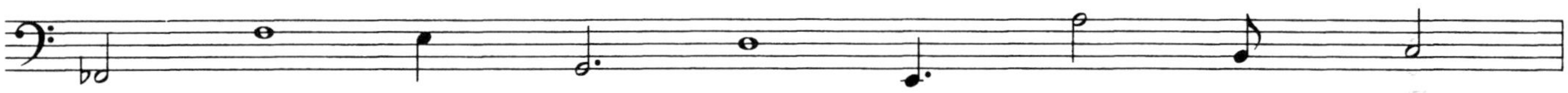

F♭ (*Example*) ....

Below are **FLATTED NOTES** as they appear on the GRAND STAFF and keyboard.

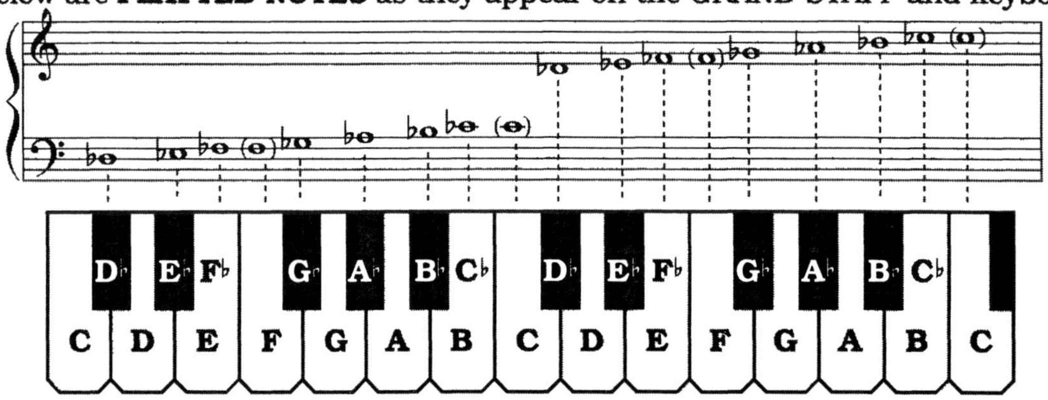

DIRECTIONS: ❶ Each keyboard below displays a pitch marked x. Circle the keyboard pitch that is a half step down from the given pitch. ❷ Draw the note on the staff directly below. Use a flat sign when necessary. ***Some examples have two possible answers.***

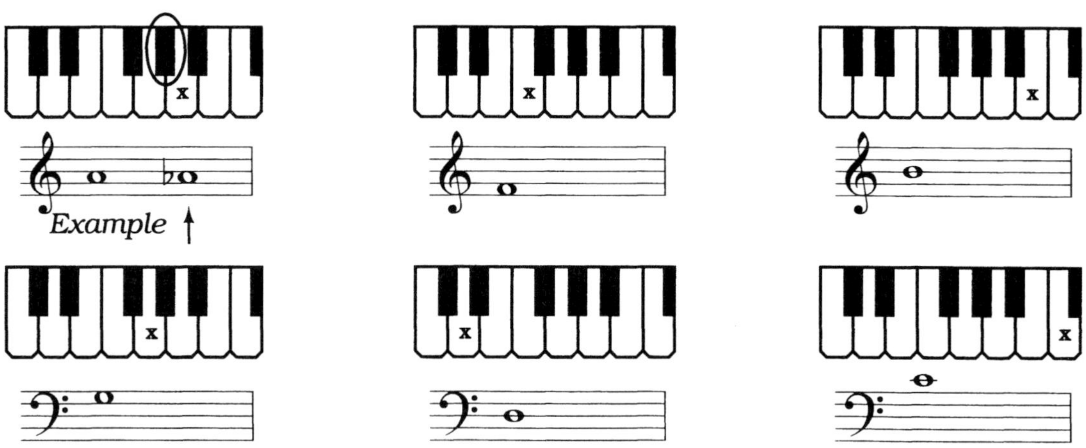

REVIEW OF LESSONS 53-56

DIRECTIONS: ❶ Circle the sharp and flat signs. ❷ Write **S** for sharp or **F** for flat above each accidental sign.

LE SECRET

Moderato *Gautier*

DIRECTIONS: Circle T for TRUE or F for FALSE.

T F 1. A half step on the keyboard is from one key to the next nearest key regardless of color.

T F 2. From one black key to the next nearest black key on the keyboard is a half step.

T F 3. Accidental signs are used to raise or lower the pitch of a note.

T F 4. A sharp or flat sign is placed after the note on the staff.

T F 5. A flat sign before a note indicates the pitch should be lowered one half step.

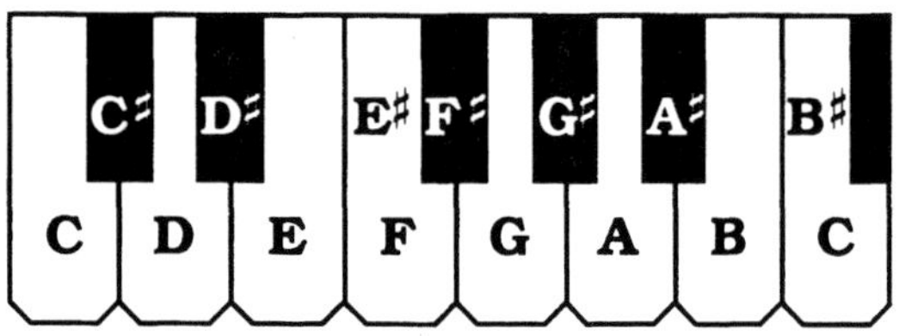

Keyboard Displaying Sharps

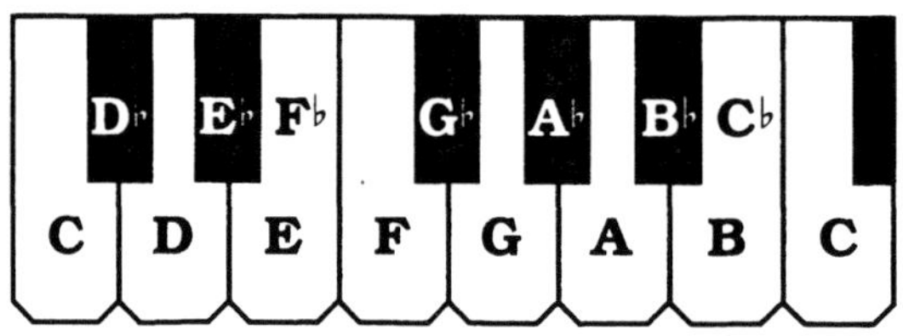

Keyboard Displaying Flats

DIRECTIONS: ❶ Each keyboard below displays a key marked x. Circle the keyboard pitch that is a half step up from the given pitch x.
❷ Draw the note on the staff directly below. Use a sharp sign when necessary. ***Some examples may have two possible answers.***

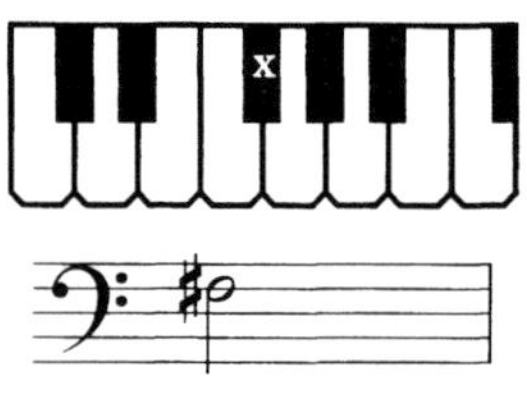

DIRECTIONS: ❶ Each keyboard below displays a pitch marked x. Circle the keyboard pitch that is a half step down from the given pitch x.
❷ Draw the note on the staff directly below. Use a flat sign when necessary. ***Some examples may have two possible answers.***

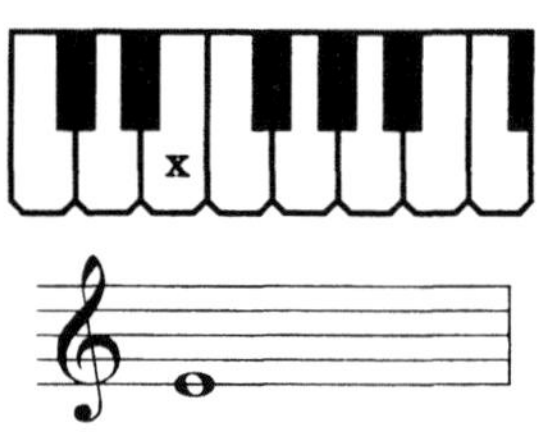

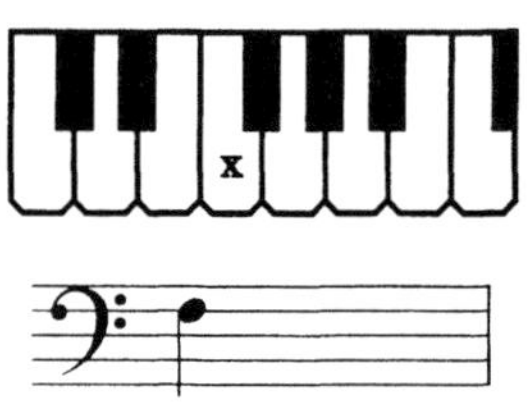

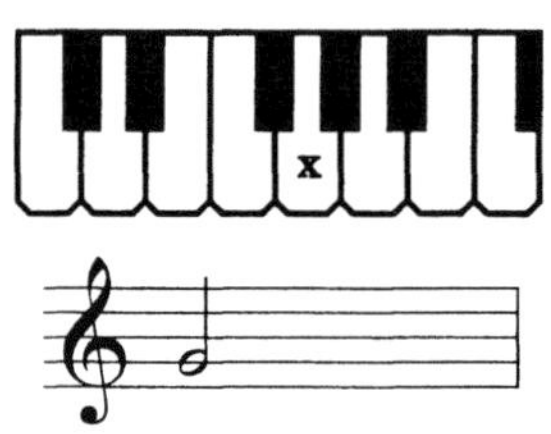

57. THE NATURAL SIGN

This ♮ is a NATURAL SIGN.

A NATURAL SIGN cancels a previous ACCIDENTAL SIGN.

DIRECTIONS: Circle the NATURALED NOTES.

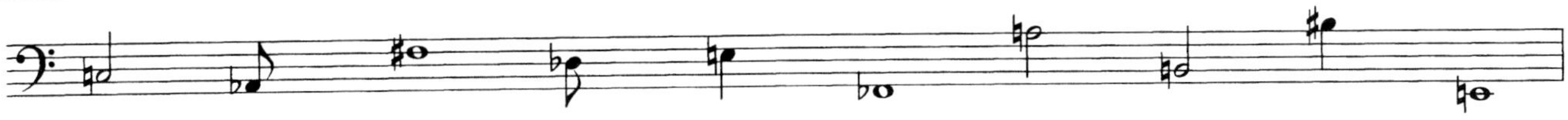

The **NATURAL SIGN** is placed before the NOTE and must be on the same LINE or SPACE as the NOTE.
*However, the **NATURAL SIGN** is placed after the LETTER NAME.* ⟶

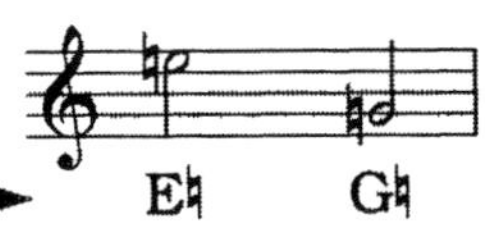

E♮ G♮

DIRECTIONS: ❶ Draw a NATURAL SIGN before each NOTE on the same LINE or SPACE. ❷ Write the LETTER NAME of each NOTE. *Include the NATURAL SIGN.*

F♮ ....
Example

A NATURAL SIGN ♮ CANCELS a previous ACCIDENTAL SIGN of the same PITCH.

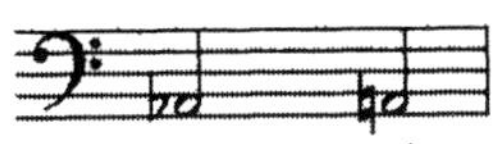

A♭ A♮

D♯ D♮

DIRECTIONS: ❶ Cancel the SHARP or FLAT in each MEASURE by placing a NATURAL SIGN in front of the second NOTE. ❷ Write the LETTER NAMES of the NOTES. ***Include the ACCIDENTAL SIGNS.***

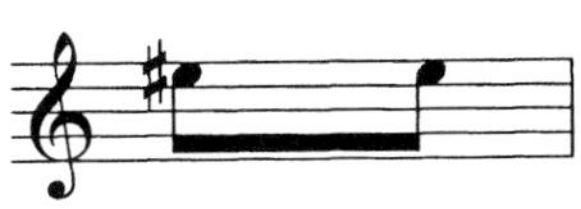

....

DIRECTIONS: ❶ Circle each NATURALED NOTE and the preceding SHARPED NOTE that it cancels. ❷ Write the LETTER NAME of each circled NOTE. ***Include the ACCIDENTAL SIGN.***

FÜR ELISE
Beethoven

....

ANDANTE
Jos. Haydn

....

58. MUSICAL STORY V

DIRECTIONS: Write the LINE or SPACE letter name of the ACCIDENTAL SIGN to form the missing words.

A DREAM COME TRUE

 and   saw an 

A ....

that read "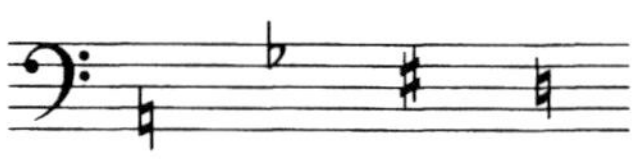 farm for sale on   end road."

....

", this is just what we've been looking for," 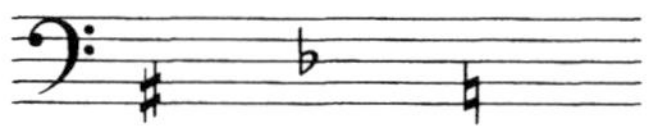 said. When they

....

arrived, they saw  cattle at the 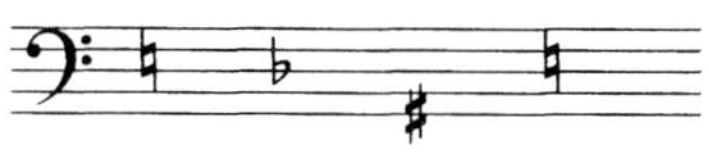 of  lake, a

....

 of flowers by 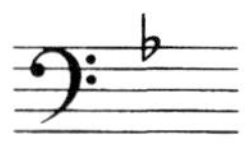  barn and an old taxi 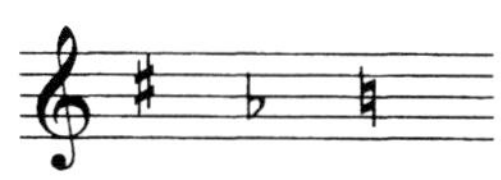

....

in the weeds.  and  were greeted by the owner, Mrs. 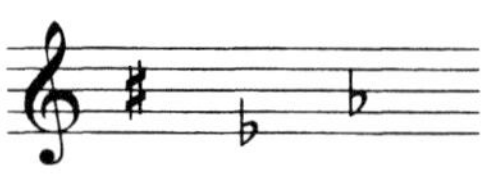

....

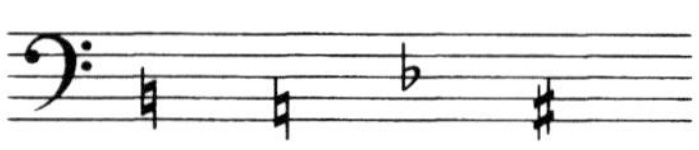. "This was originally   farm," she said.

....

"My late husband paid 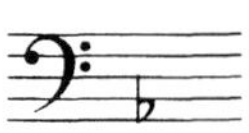 big price for the place," she 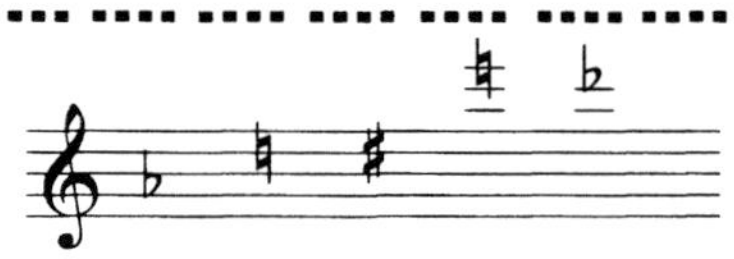.

....

"Mrs.  and I would like to buy it," said . "Very well, " said Mrs.

....

. "My lawyer has the ." Ed had a smile on his

....

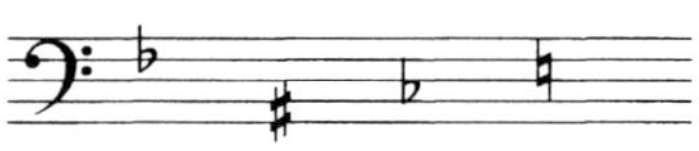 as they closed the deal.  lifelong dream had come true.

....

59. MORE ABOUT ACCIDENTALS

WRITING HALF STEPS ON THE STAFF

These are examples of how HALF STEPS are written on the STAFF using ACCIDENTAL SIGNS.

G♭ G♮	A A♯	E D♯	F♭ E♭
HALF STEP UP ↑	*HALF STEP UP* ↑	*HALF STEP DOWN* ↓	*HALF STEP DOWN* ↓

DIRECTIONS: ❶ Write the LETTER NAMES of the NOTES plus the ACCIDENTAL SIGNS for each of the examples.
❷ Circle **U** for HALF STEP UP or **D** for HALF STEP DOWN.

U **B♭ A**
Ⓓ *Example*

U D ....

U D ....

U D ....

U D ....

An ACCIDENTAL SIGN ♯ ♭ ♮ only affects a NOTE for one MEASURE.

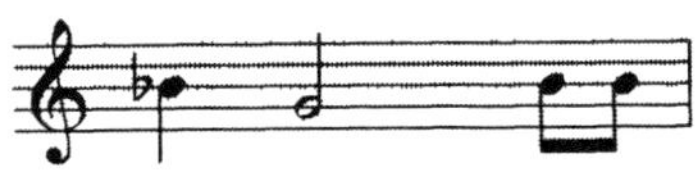

Written → *Actually performed* →

ACCIDENTALS actually performed

DIRECTIONS: Draw ACCIDENTAL SIGNS in the second MEASURE of each example as needed to show what SHARPS, FLATS and NATURALS should actually be performed.

1. 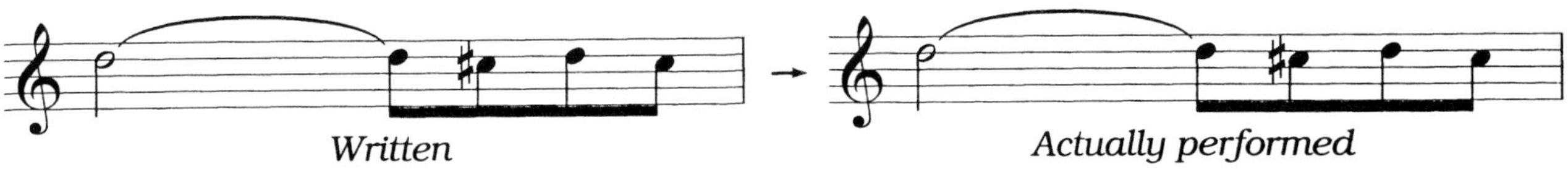

Written → *Actually performed*

2. 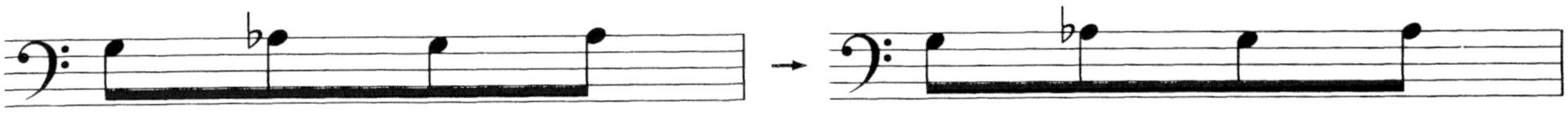

Written → *Actually performed*

3. 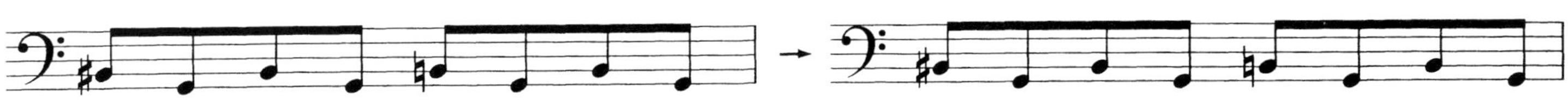

Written → *Actually performed*

60. THE WHOLE STEP AND ENHARMONIC PITCHES

A **WHOLE STEP** consists of TWO HALF STEPS.
*On the keyboard a **WHOLE STEP** consists of three consecutive keys regardless of color.*

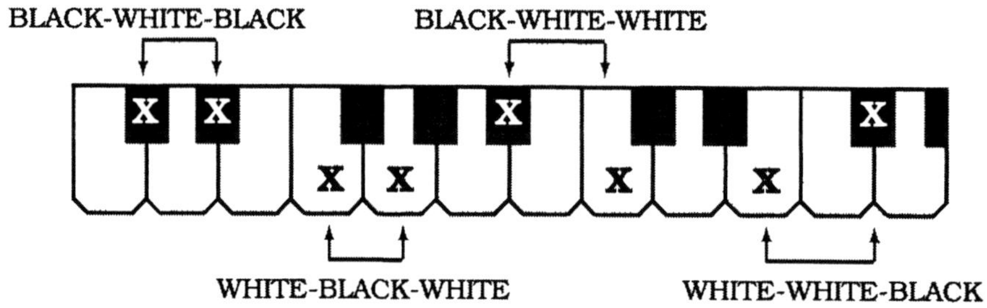

DIRECTIONS: Circle the keyboards that display a WHOLE STEP.

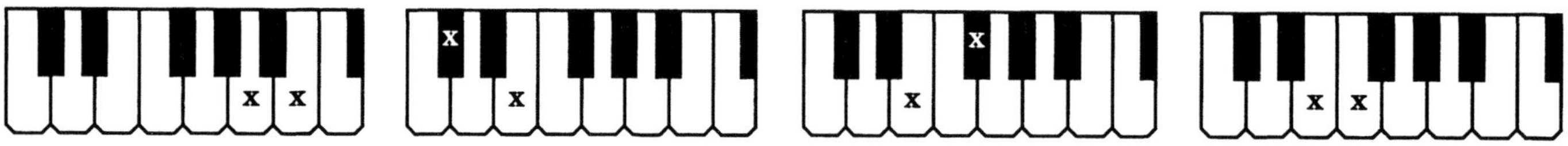

DIRECTIONS: ❶ Each keyboard below displays a WHOLE STEP. The first NOTE of each WHOLE STEP is given on the STAFF. ❷ Add the second NOTE of the WHOLE STEP. ❸ Write the LETTER NAMES of the NOTES on the dotted lines.

1. 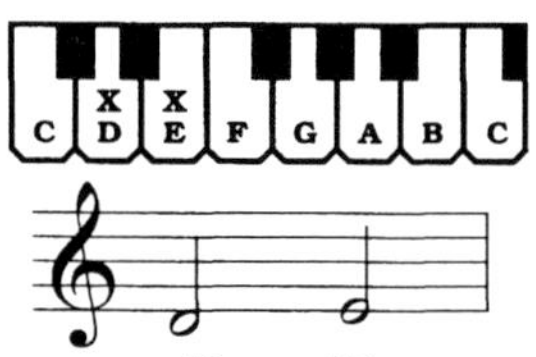

D E ....
Example

2. 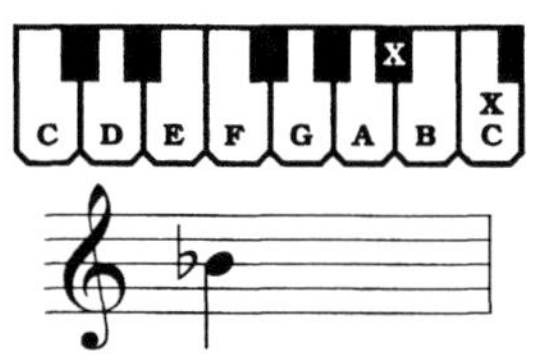

....

3. 

....

4. 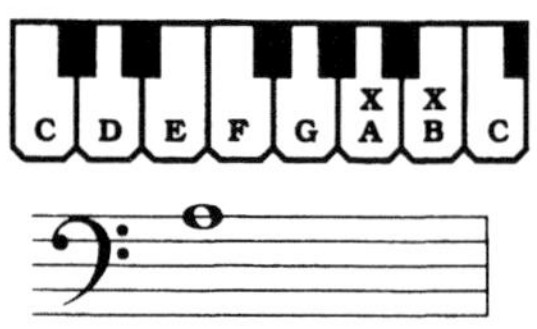

....

5. 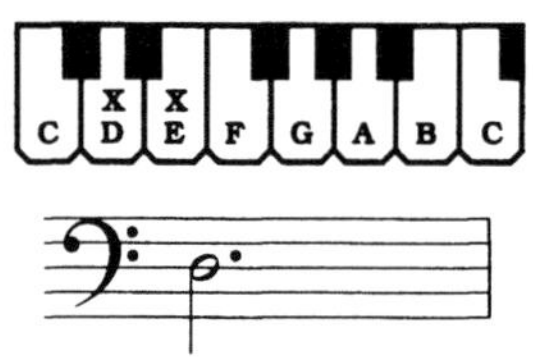

....

6. 

....

ENHARMONIC PITCHES

Some PITCHES can be written two different ways. For example:

 → *has the same sound as* → 

G♯ → *is the same as* → **A♭**

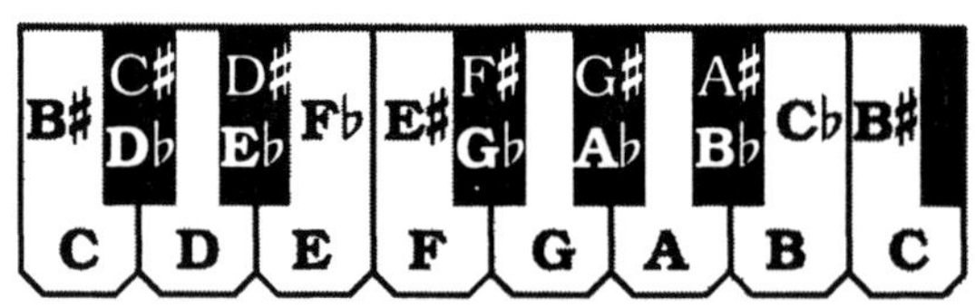

ENHARMONIC KEYBOARD PITCH (NOTE) CHART

PITCHES that sound the same but are written differently are called **ENHARMONIC**.

DIRECTIONS: ❶ Draw the ENHARMONIC NOTES of the following PITCHES. ❷ Write the LETTER NAMES of the ENHARMONIC NOTES. ***Include the ACCIDENTAL SIGNS.***

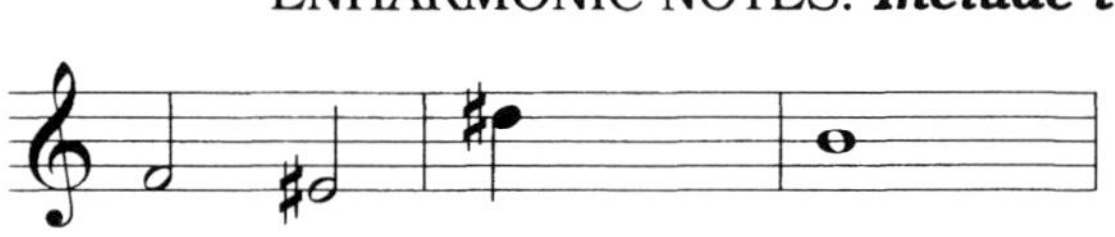

F E♯ ....
Example

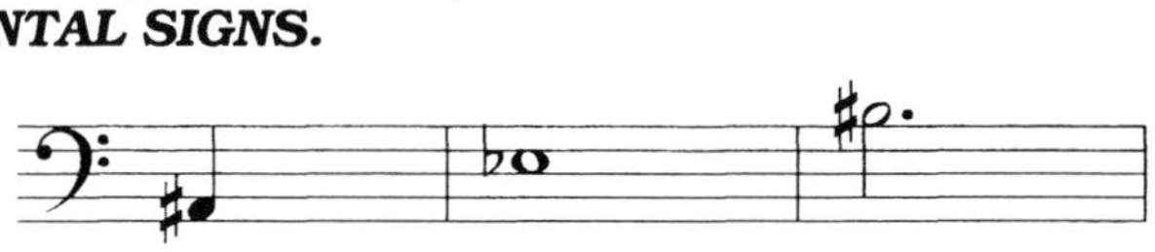

....

REVIEW OF LESSONS 57-60

DIRECTIONS: Match each description on the left with the best example on the right.

_____ Sharp sign

_____ Half Step

_____ Enharmonic note of A♭

_____ Flat sign

_____ Whole step

_____ Accidental signs

_____ Natural sign

A. 

B. 

C. 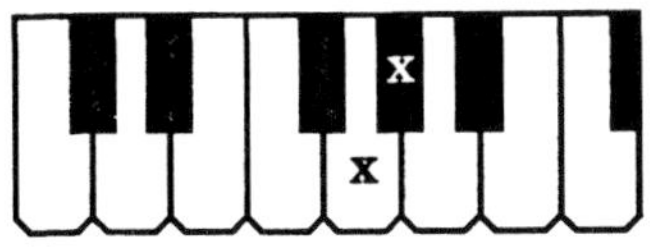

D. 

E. 

F. 

G. 

DIRECTIONS: Circle each natural sign and the preceding sharp or flat sign that it cancels.

FUGUE IN D MINOR

Pachelbel

QUARTET IN B FLAT (3rd Mov.)

Brahms

DIRECTIONS: Draw accidental signs in the second measure as needed to show how the notes should actually be performed.

TRICKY TRICKS

DePaul

Written

→

Actually performed

DIRECTIONS: Each keyboard and staff display a pitch. Draw the enharmonic note of the pitch on the staff.

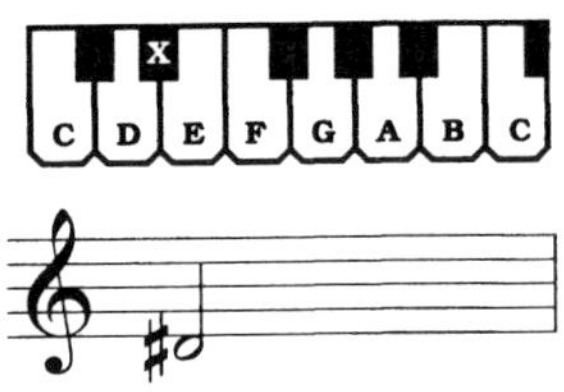

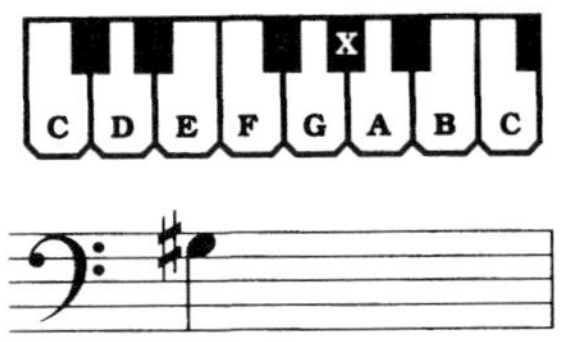

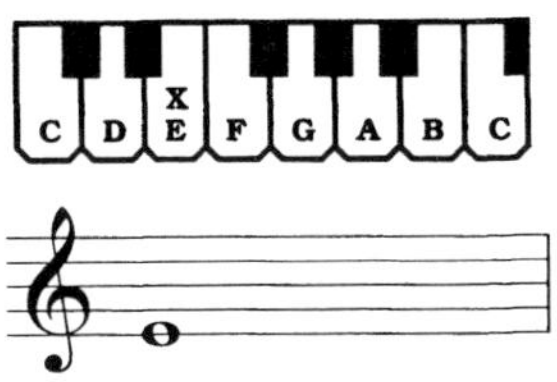

DIRECTIONS: ❶ Each keyboard below displays either a half or whole step. Circle **H** for a half step or **W** for a whole step. ❷ Use notes of your choice to draw the keyboard pitches on the staff. ***Some examples have more than one answer.*** ❸ Write the letter names of the notes, plus accidental signs if needed, on the dotted lines. ***Some examples may require a natural sign before the second note.***

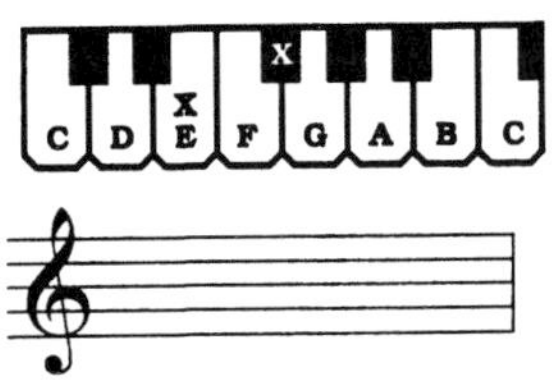

H
W ....

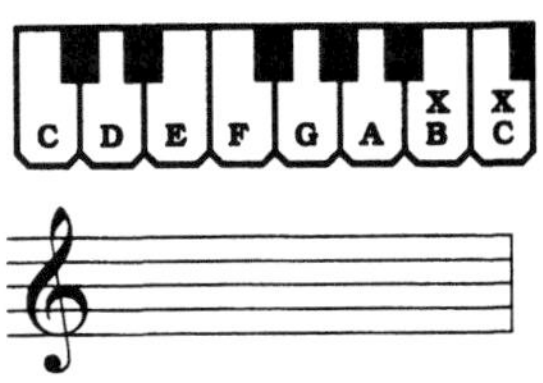

H
W ....

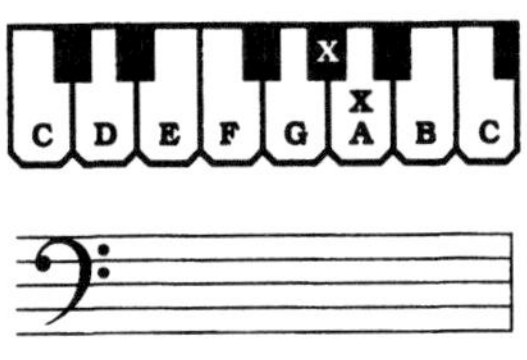

H
W ....

H
W ....

61. SCALES

A **SCALE** is a series of PITCHES arranged like a ladder in a particular order.
These are examples of **SCALES**.

(C) D E F G A B (C)

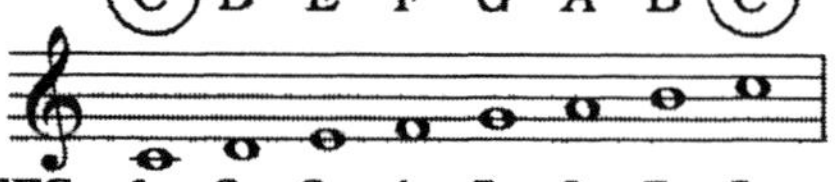

DEGREES: 1 2 3 4 5 6 7 8

(F) E D C B♭ A G (F)

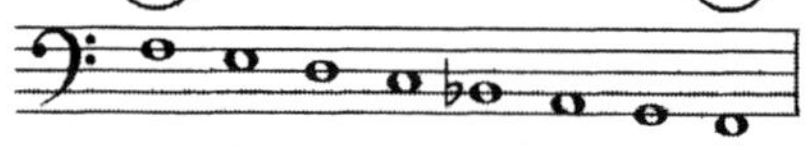

8 7 6 5 4 3 2 1

(C) D E G A (C)

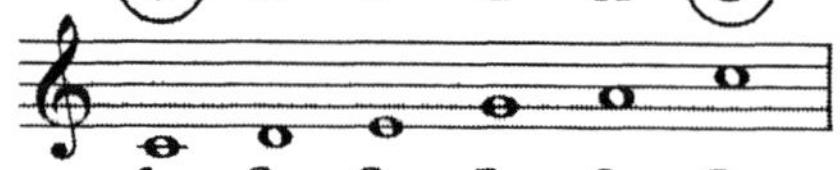

1 2 3 5 6 8

Most **SCALES** have eight **DEGREES** (NOTES), the first and last **DEGREES** (1 & 8) having the same LETTER NAME.
Some ***SCALES*** *have fewer than eight* ***DEGREES****. Others have more.*

DIRECTIONS: Circle the letter of the music examples that display a SCALE.

A. 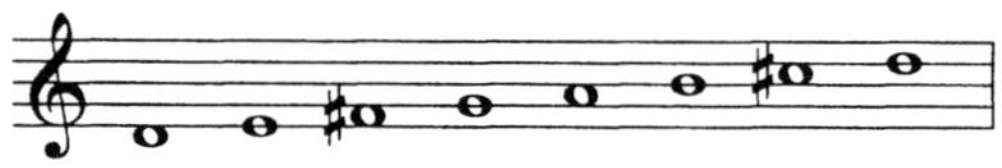

B. 

C. 

D. 

SCALES ASCEND (move upward) and DESCEND (move downward).

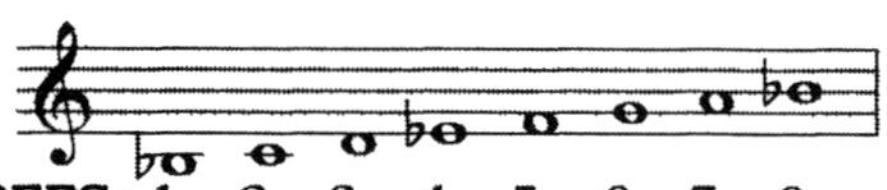

DEGREES: 1 2 3 4 5 6 7 8

ASCENDING SCALE

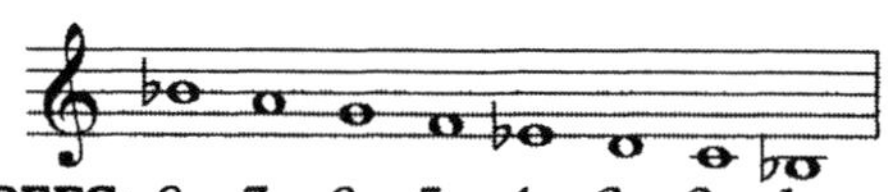

DEGREES: 8 7 6 5 4 3 2 1

DESCENDING SCALE

DIRECTIONS: Identify each SCALE as ASCENDING or DESCENDING.

....

....

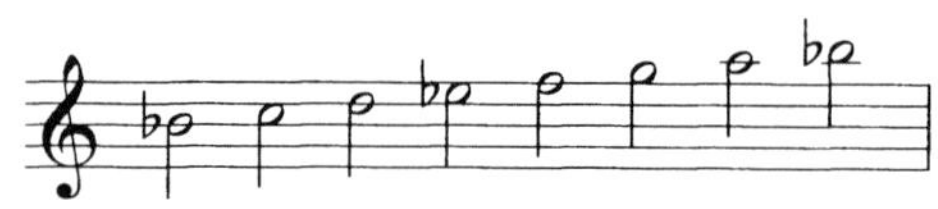

....

DIRECTIONS: ❶ Draw the following ASCENDING and DESCENDING SCALES. Each SCALE should have eight STEPWISE NOTES. ❷ Write the DEGREE numbers for each SCALE. ***The beginning NOTE and DEGREE number are given.***

ASCENDING

DEGREES: **1** ....

DESCENDING

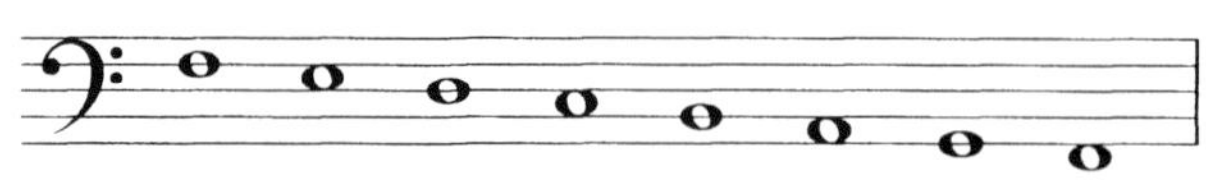

DEGREES: **8** ....

DESCENDING

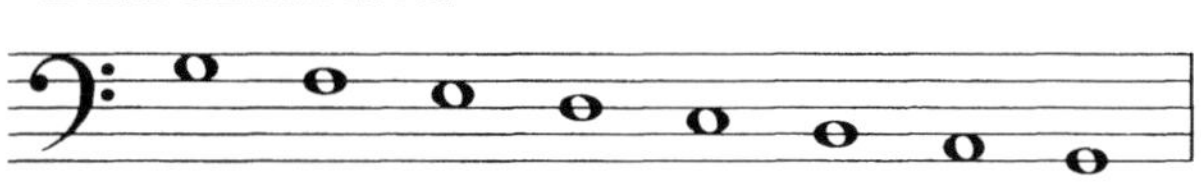

DEGREES: **8** ....

ASCENDING

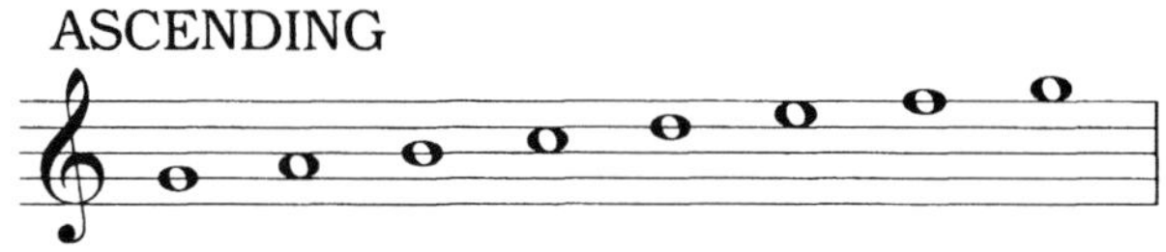

DEGREES: **1** ....

62. CONSTRUCTING MAJOR SCALES AND THE C MAJOR SCALE

These are **MAJOR SCALES**.

DEGREES: 1 2 3 4 5 6 7 8

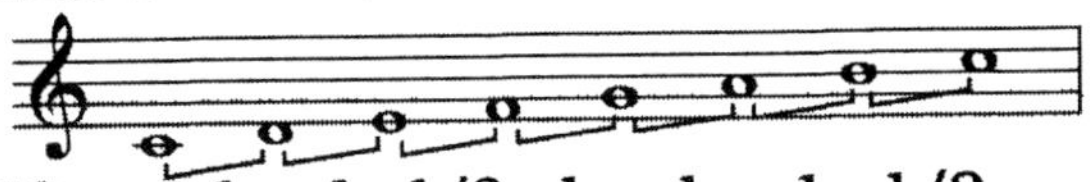

STEPS: 1 1 1/2 1 1 1 1/2

ASCENDING C MAJOR SCALE

DEGREES: 1 2 3 4 5 6 7 8

STEPS: 1 1 1/2 1 1 1 1/2

ASCENDING G MAJOR SCALE

*ALL **MAJOR SCALES** are constructed according to a specific pattern.*

RULE: HALF STEPS occur between the 3rd and 4th and the 7th and 8th DEGREES of the **MAJOR SCALE**. All the other STEPS are WHOLE STEPS.

DIRECTIONS: Complete the following sentences about the MAJOR SCALE.

1. A MAJOR SCALE has ________ DEGREES.
2. A MAJOR SCALE has ________ WHOLE STEPS and ______ HALF STEPS.
3. HALF STEPS occur between the _____ and _____ and the _____ and _____ DEGREES.

This is the **C MAJOR SCALE**.

DEGREES: 1 2 3 4 5 6 7 8
C D E F G A B C

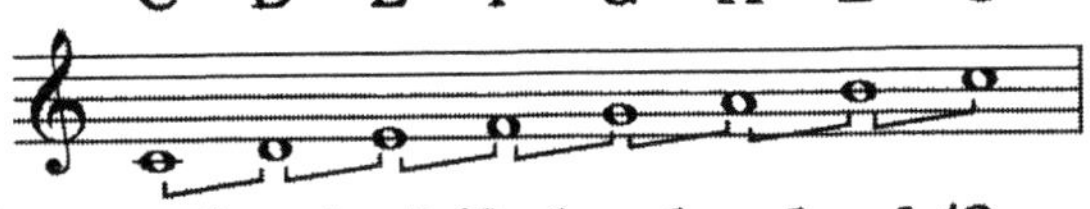

STEPS: 1 1 1/2 1 1 1 1/2

C MAJOR SCALE *(ASCENDING)*

DEGREES: 8 7 6 5 4 3 2 1
C B A G F E D C

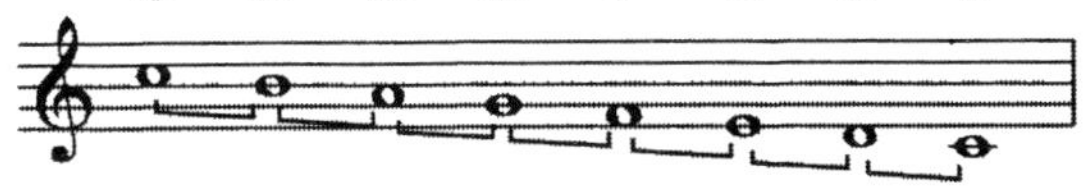

STEPS: 1/2 1 1 1 1/2 1 1

C MAJOR SCALE *(DESCENDING)*

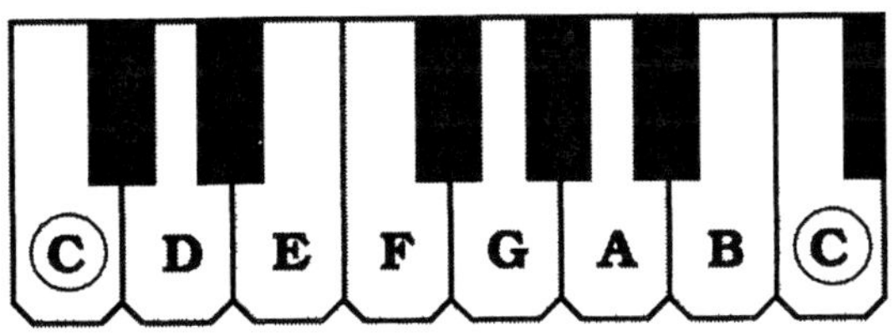

*The **C MAJOR SCALE** begins and ends on C and has no SHARPS, FLATS or NATURALS.*

DIRECTIONS: Below are several MAJOR SCALES in both the TREBLE and BASS CLEF. Circle the C MAJOR SCALES.

1. 

2. 

3. 

4. 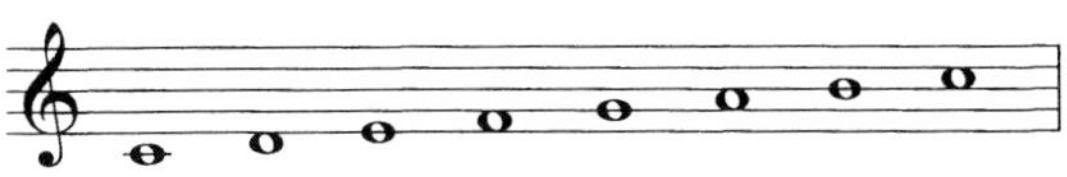

DIRECTIONS: ❶ Draw the C MAJOR SCALE (ASCENDING and DESCENDING) on the BASS CLEF STAFF.
❷ Write the DEGREE numbers above the STAFF and the STEP numbers below the STAFF.

DEGREES: **1 2** ....

STEPS: **1** ....

DEGREES: **8 7** ....

STEPS: **1/2** ....

63. THE TONIC NOTE AND KEY SIGNATURES

The **TONIC NOTE*** is the first DEGREE of a MAJOR SCALE.

***TONIC** LETTER NAME* → Ⓒ D E F G A B C

TONIC NOTE →

DEGREES → 1 2 3 4 5 6 7 8

C MAJOR SCALE

*The **TONIC NOTE** is the **strongest** and most **important** NOTE in the MAJOR SCALE.*

*Also known as the **KEY NOTE**, **HOME TONE**, **DO**, **KEY CENTER**.

DIRECTIONS: Write in the box the name of the TONIC NOTE for each MAJOR SCALE.

1. [D] *Example*

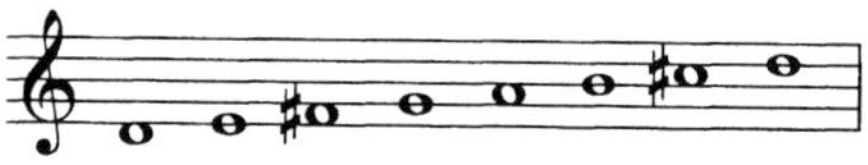

2. [ ]

3. [ ]

4. [ ]

5. [ ]

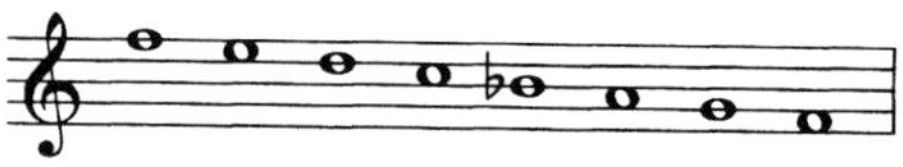

6. [ ]

These

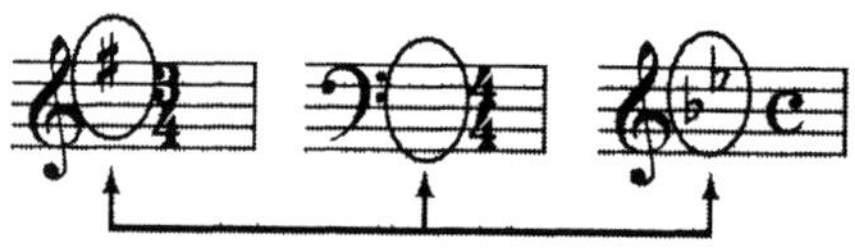

are KEY SIGNATURES

***KEY SIGNATURE** area*

*The **KEY SIGNATURE** area is found at the beginning of a piece of music between the CLEF SIGN and the TIME SIGNATURE.*

DIRECTIONS: Circle the KEY SIGNATURE areas.

BINGO *Scotland*

SHORT'NIN' BREAD *U.S.*

NOW THANK WE ALL OUR GOD *Crüger*

DIRECTIONS: ❶ Find and circle the notes of the ASCENDING C MAJOR SCALE (eight NOTES).

❷ Can you name this famous English carol? ____________________

64. THE KEY OF C MAJOR AND THE $\frac{6}{8}$ TIME SIGNATURE

This is the KEY of **C MAJOR.** →

The KEY SIGNATURE of **C MAJOR** *indicates:*

1. *The music will be based on the DEGREES of the* **C MAJOR SCALE.**
2. *The TONIC NOTE is C. (No SHARPS or FLATS in the KEY SIGNATURE)*

DIRECTIONS: Circle the examples that are in the KEY of C MAJOR.

GOOD NIGHT, LADIES
College Song

ON TOP OF OLD SMOKY
American

LITTLE PRELUDE
Bach

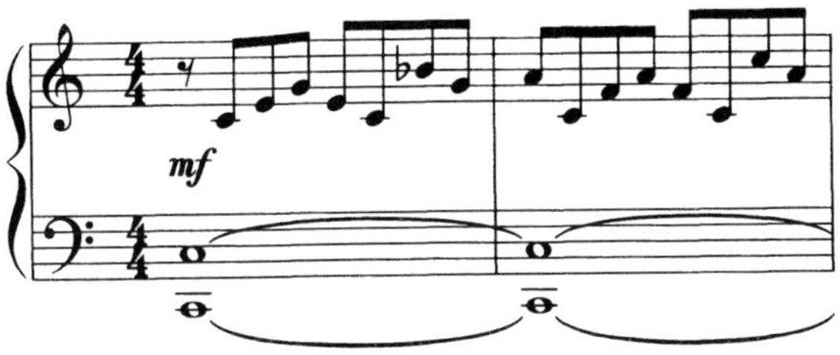

SUNSET AND EVENING STAR
Parry

THE $\frac{6}{8}$ TIME SIGNATURE

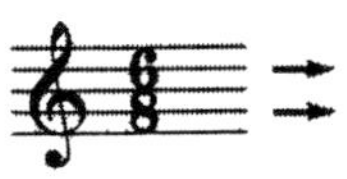

→ *SIX (6) BEATS in each MEASURE*
→ *EIGHTH NOTE (♪) gets ONE (1) BEAT (PULSE)*

NOTE VALUES IN $\frac{6}{8}$ *TIME*

♪ = 1 ♩ = 2 ♩. = 3 𝅗𝅥. = 6

DIRECTIONS: Write the number of BEATS for each NOTE in $\frac{6}{8}$ TIME.

Steadily **ROW, ROW, ROW YOUR BOAT** *Unknown*

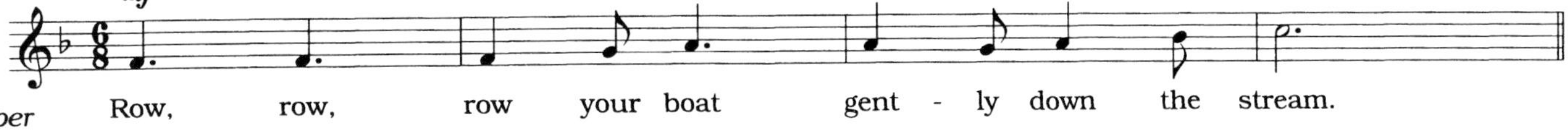

Number of beats → ....

REVIEW OF LESSONS 61-64

DIRECTIONS: Complete each sentence below with one of the words in the box.

DOWNWARD	**KEY**	**THREE**	**WHOLE**	**UPWARD**
EIGHT	**PATTERN**	**SCALE**	**ONE**	**TONIC NOTE**

1. A ______________________ is a series of pitches arranged in a particular order.
2. An ascending scale moves ______________________ .
3. A descending scale moves ______________________ .
4. All major scales are constructed according to a specific ______________________ .
5. Most scales have ______________________ degrees (notes).
6. The strongest and most important note in a scale is the ______________________ .
7. A major scale has half steps between the 3rd and 4th and 7th and 8th degrees. All the other steps are ______________________ steps.
8. The __________ signature is found at the beginning of each music system.
9. In $\frac{6}{8}$ time an eighth note gets ____________ beat(s).
10. In $\frac{6}{8}$ time a dotted quarter note gets ____________ beat(s).

DIRECTIONS: ❶ Draw the ascending and descending scales of C major on the treble staff. ❷ Write the degree numbers below the staff.

C MAJOR (ASCENDING)

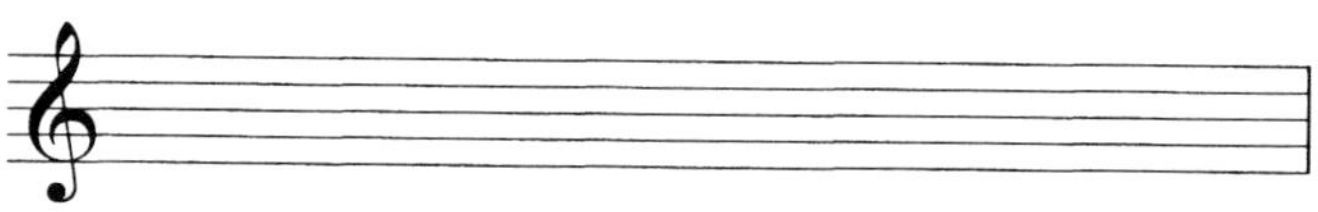

DEGREES → **1** ....

C MAJOR (DESCENDING)

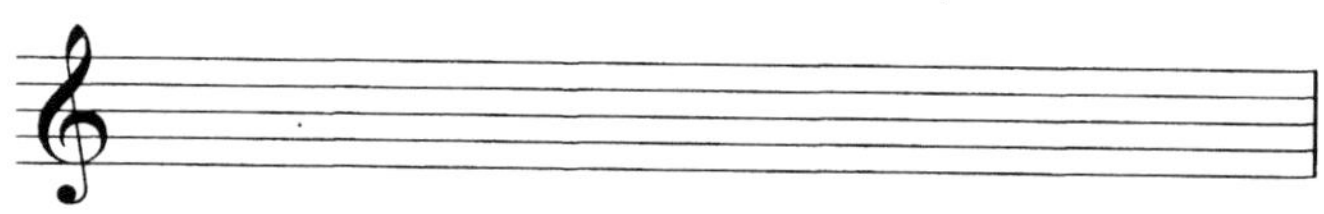

DEGREES → **8** ....

DIRECTIONS: Some of the half and whole step numbers are missing for the C major scales below. Write in the missing numbers.

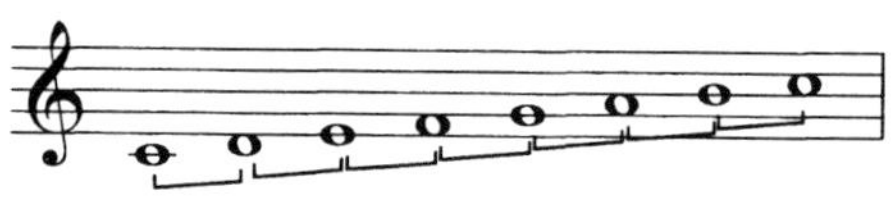

STEPS → **1 1 1 1 1/2**

STEPS → **1 1 1/2 1**

DIRECTIONS: Study the Dietrich Buxtehude organ piece and then answer the questions.

FUGUE

Buxtehude

1. *FUGUE* is in the key of _______ major. Write an **X** in the key signature area.
2. How many beats are in each measure? ______________________
3. What kind of note gets one beat? ______________________

   BONUS: Circle the notes and rests of the entire alto part.

65. THE KEY OF G MAJOR AND COUNTING IN $\frac{6}{8}$ TIME

This is the KEY SIGNATURE of **G MAJOR** ⟶

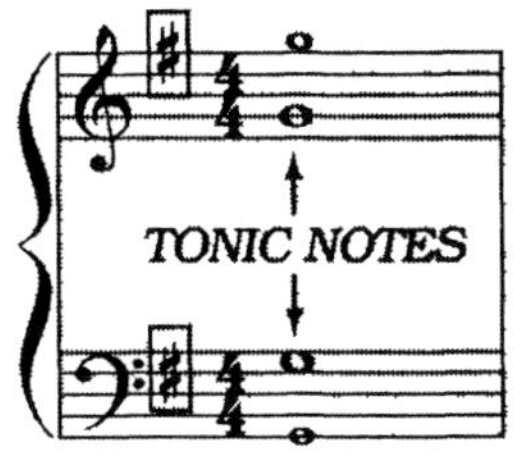

The KEY SIGNATURE of **G MAJOR** *indicates:*

1. *The music will be based on the DEGREES of the* **G MAJOR SCALE.**
2. *The TONIC NOTE is G.*

DIRECTIONS: Circle the music examples that are in the KEY of G MAJOR.

ANGELS WE HAVE HEARD ON HIGH
French

RONDO A CAPRICCIO
Beethoven

MISTER FROG
Traditional

SHARPS or FLATS in the KEY SIGNATURE indicate which NOTES will be SHARPED or FLATTED for the *entire composition.*

ALL THROUGH THE NIGHT
British

Written

⟶

Actually performed

The F♯ *in the KEY SIGNATURE indicates that all* F's ANYWHERE *in the* ENTIRE COMPOSITION *must be* SHARPED.

DIRECTIONS: Below is *RONDO* in the KEY of G MAJOR. Find all the F's and SHARP each one to indicate how the music should actually be performed.

RONDO
Clementi

Study how the music below is COUNTED in $\frac{6}{8}$ *TIME.*

DRINK TO ME ONLY WITH THINE EYES
Steadily
English

COUNTS ⟶	1	2	3	4	5	6	1	2	3	4	5	6
No. of BEATS ⟶	(1)	(1)	(1)	(1)	(1)	(1)	(1)	(1)	(1)	(1)	(1)	(1)

DIRECTIONS: Write the COUNTING on the dotted line.

SWEET AND LOW
Barnby

COUNT & write ⟶ ....

66. THE KEYS OF G, D AND A MAJOR AND 6/8 TIME COUNTED IN TWO

HOW TO IDENTIFY KEY SIGNATURES WITH SHARPS

RULE: The name of a MAJOR SHARP KEY can be determined by moving one DEGREE up from the last SHARP to the right in the KEY SIGNATURE.

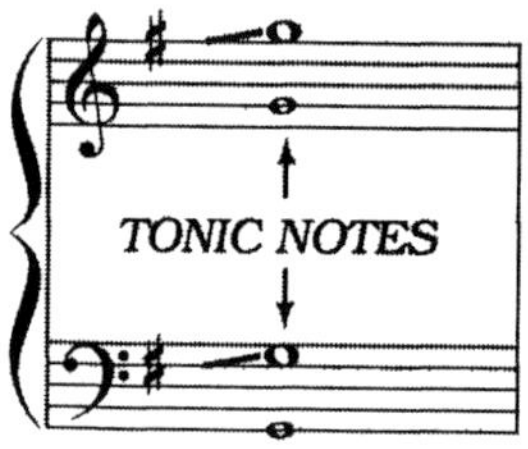

KEY of G MAJOR

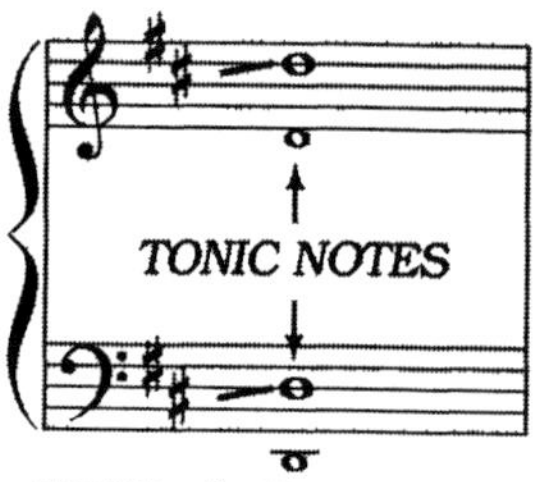

KEY of D MAJOR

KEY of A MAJOR

DIRECTIONS: Study each KEY SIGNATURE and then write in the box the MAJOR KEY name for each piece of music. ***Be sure to include the word MAJOR (MAJ.).***

TO A WILD ROSE

MacDowell

MEET ME IN ST. LOUIE

Mills

GIVE MY REGARDS TO BROADWAY

Cohan

MINUET

Mozart

Music in 6/8 TIME with a quick TEMPO is COUNTED and CONDUCTED TWO (2) BEATS (PULSES) to a MEASURE.

A DOTTED QUARTER NOTE (♩.) get ONE (1) BEAT (PULSE) in 6/8 TIME.

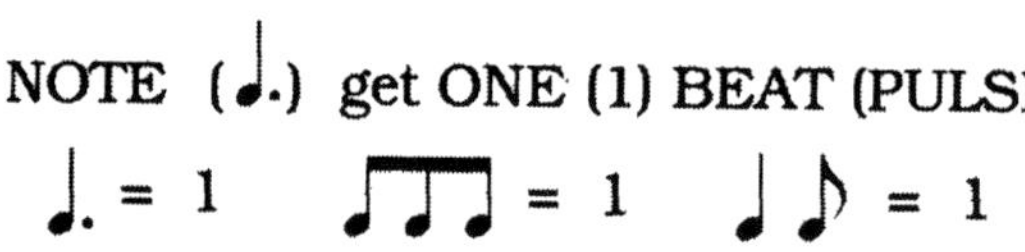

Animated **OVER THE RIVER AND THROUGH THE WOODS**

U.S.

COUNTS →	1	2	1	2	1	2
No. of BEATS →	(1)	(1)	(1)	(1)	(1)	(1)

DIRECTIONS: Write the COUNTING on the dotted line.

Quickly **POP! GOES THE WEASEL**

U.S.

COUNT & write → 1 2 ....

Example

67. THE KEY OF F MAJOR AND THE $\frac{2}{2}$ OR ¢ TIME SIGNATURE

This is the KEY SIGNATURE of **F MAJOR.** ⟶

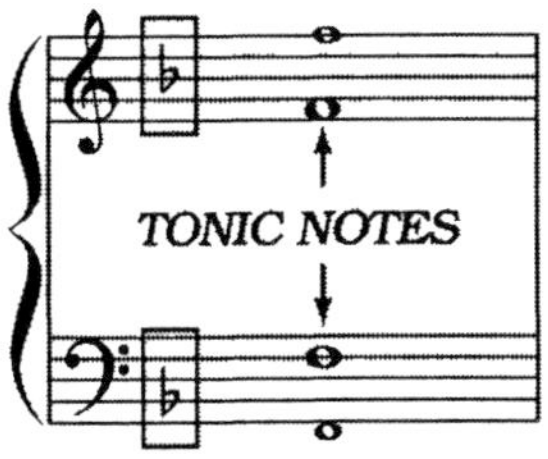

The KEY SIGNATURE of ***F MAJOR*** *indicates:*
1. *The music will be based on the DEGREES of the* ***F MAJOR SCALE.***
2. *The TONIC NOTE is F.*

DIRECTIONS: ❶ Circle the examples that are in the KEY of F MAJOR. ❷ Find all the B's in the F MAJOR examples and FLAT each one to show how the music should actually be performed.

WHEN THE SAINTS GO MARCHING IN *Spiritual*

THE BAND PLAYED ON *Ward*

SPINNING SONG *Ellmenreich*

THE $\frac{2}{2}$ or ¢ TIME SIGNATURE

 → *TWO (2) BEATS in each MEASURE*
→ *HALF NOTE (𝅗𝅥) gets ONE (1) BEAT (PULSE)*

This  is the **CUT TIME*** SIGN.

CUT TIME  *is the same as*  *TIME.*

NOTE VALUES IN $\frac{2}{2}$ or ¢ TIME

𝅝 = 2 𝅗𝅥. = 1 1/2 𝅗𝅥 = 1 ♩ = 1/2 ♪ = 1/4

* Also known as the ALLA BREVE SIGN

DIRECTIONS: Write the number of BEATS for each NOTE in $\frac{2}{2}$ TIME.

HEY, HO, NOBODY AT HOME

Moderato *English*

No. of BEATS → ....

68. THE KEYS OF F, B♭ AND E♭ MAJOR AND COUNTING IN $\frac{2}{2}$ OR ¢ TIME

RULE:

HOW TO IDENTIFY KEY SIGNATURES WITH FLATS

The name of a MAJOR FLAT KEY can be determined by counting four DEGREES *DOWN* from the last FLAT to the right in the KEY SIGNATURE, always COUNTING the last FLAT as "1".

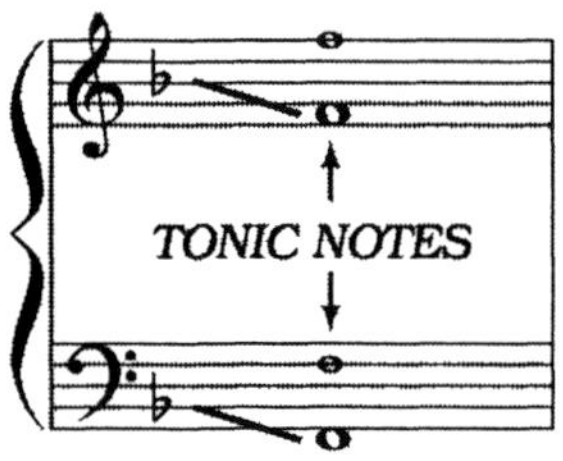

Key of ***F MAJOR***

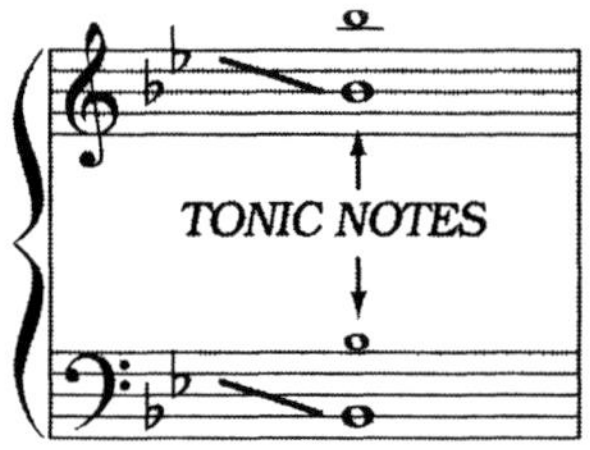

Key of ***B♭ MAJOR***

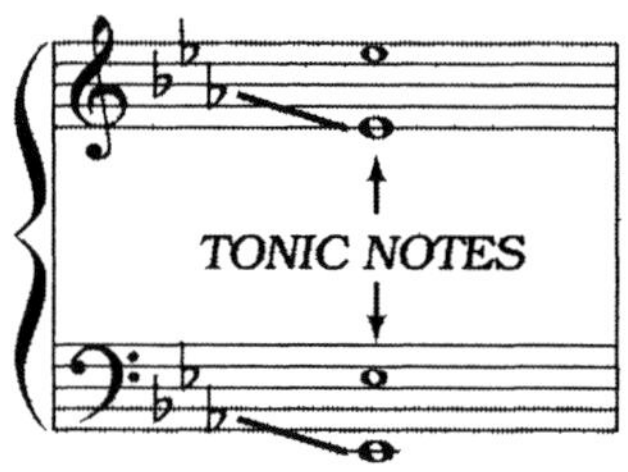

Key of ***E♭ MAJOR***

DIRECTIONS: Circle the KEY SIGNATURE area(s) and then write the KEY name in the box for each music example. Be sure to include the word MAJOR (MAJ.) and when necessary a FLAT SIGN.

ANDANTE

Clementi

GOOD NIGHT, FAREWELL

Kucken

LITTLE BROWN JUG

Traditional

SLEEP, BABY, SLEEP

German

Study how the music below is COUNTED in $\frac{2}{2}$ TIME.

SKIP TO MY LOU

Lively

U.S.

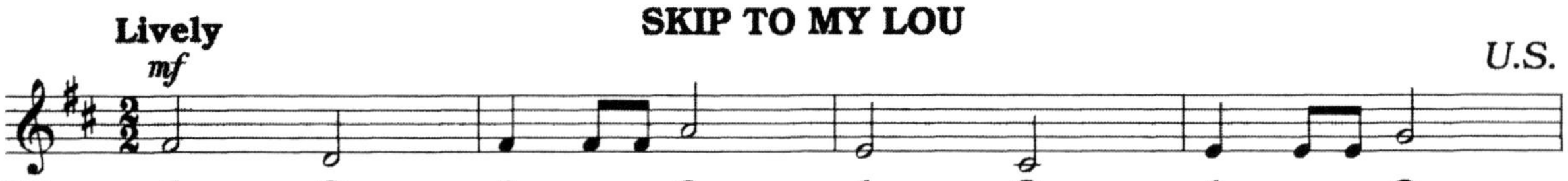

COUNTS →	1	2	1	2	1	2	1	2
No. of BEATS →	(1)	(1)	(1)	(1)	(1)	(1)	(1)	(1)

DIRECTIONS: Write the COUNTING on the dotted line.

THIS OLD MAN

Moderato

U.S.

COUNT & write → 1 2 ....

Example

REVIEW OF LESSONS 65-68

DIRECTIONS: Match each major key name from the list with the proper music example below and then write the key name in the box.

C Major **B♭ Major** **E♭ Major** **D Major** **A Major**

1. ☐ **HOME, SWEET HOME**

Bishop

4. ☐ **LITTLE ANNIE ROONEY**

Nolan

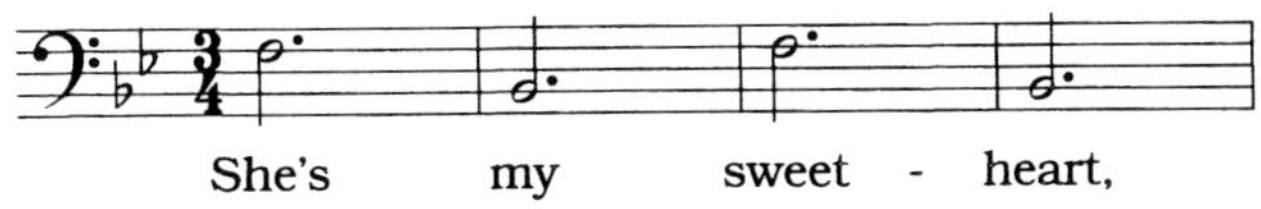

2. ☐ **LIFT THINE EYES**

Mendelssohn

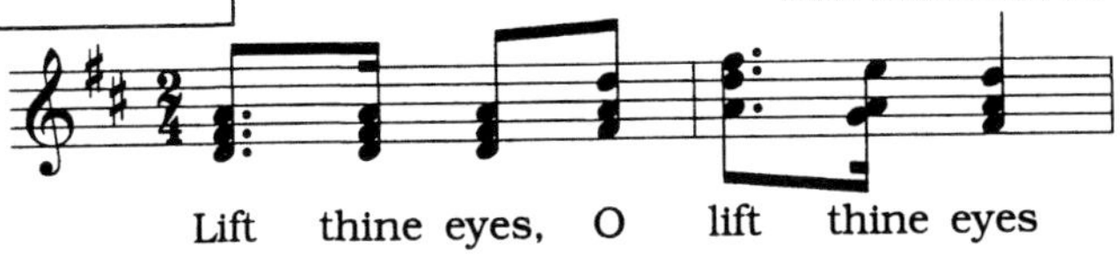

5. ☐ **THE BELLS**

Byrd

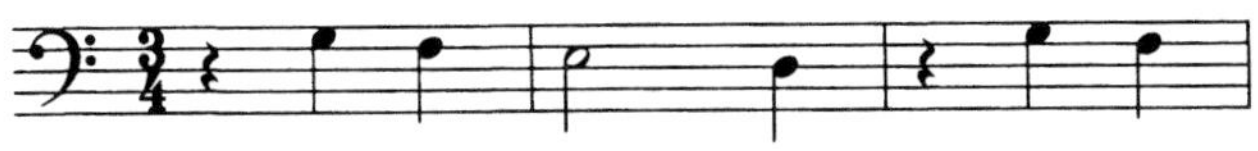

3. ☐ **PRELUDE, Op. 28, No. 1**

Chopin

DIRECTIONS: ❶ Write the key of each song in the box. ❷ Draw sharps and flats before notes as needed to show how the melody is actually performed. ❸ Study the time signature and tempo marking and then write the counting on the dotted lines. *Do not divide the beats.*

☐ **Moderato** **OLD CHISHOLM TRAIL**

U.S.

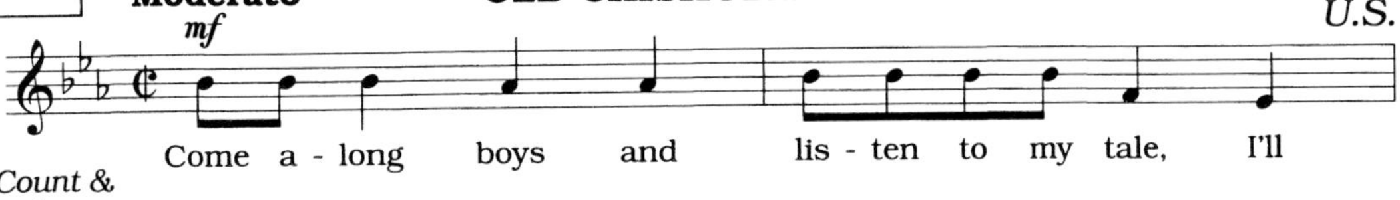

Count & write → ....

☐ **Slowly** **BLOW THE WINDS SOUTHERLY**

English

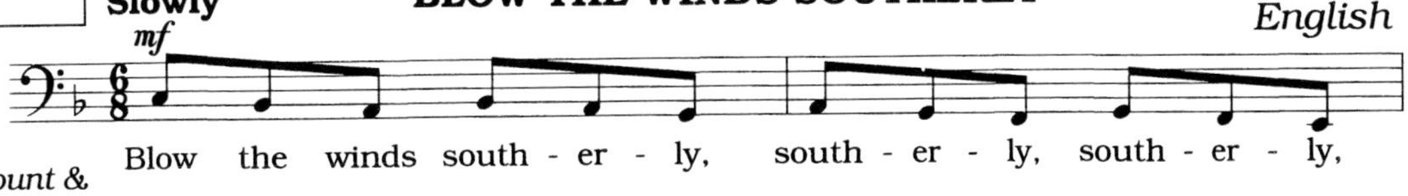

Count & write → ....

☐ **Quickly** **DOWN IN A COAL MINE**

Geoghegen

Count & write → ....

69. CHORDS AND TRIADS

There are **CHORDS**.
*A **CHORD** is THREE or MORE PITCHES sounding HARMONICALLY.*

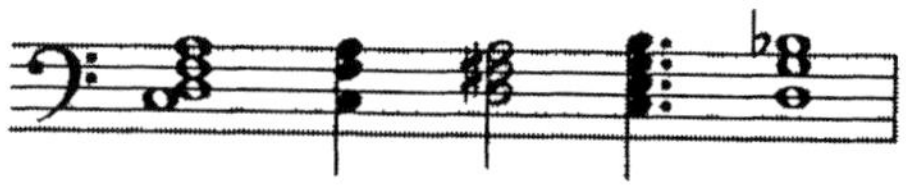

DIRECTIONS: Circle the examples that are CHORDS.

CHORDS can provide an **ACCOMPANIMENT** to a MELODY.
Study how the following MELODY is **ACCOMPANIED** in three DIFFERENT STYLES.

BLOCK CHORD STYLE

BROKEN CHORD STYLE

ARPEGGIO STYLE *(Each NOTE of the **CHORD** played separately)*

DIRECTIONS: Write the CHORD STYLE (BLOCK, BROKEN or ARPEGGIO) for Henry Purcell's *PASSING BY.*

CHORD STYLE → ....

These **CHORDS** 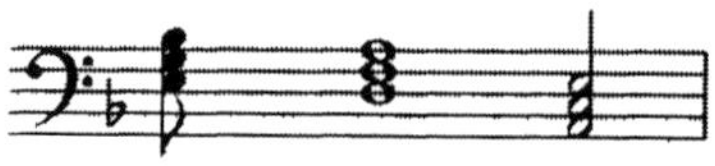 are examples of **TRIADS**.

*A **TRIAD** is a **CHORD** with THREE NOTES.*

DIRECTIONS: Circle the TRIADS.

70. MAJOR TRIADS

A **MAJOR TRIAD** (CHORD) consists of the 1ST (ROOT), 3RD and 5TH NOTES of the MAJOR SCALE.
*The **ROOT** of the **MAJOR TRIAD** is the name of the CHORD.*

C MAJOR SCALE

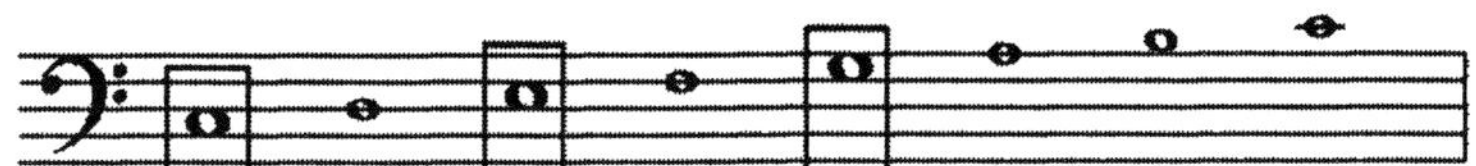

C	D	E	F	G	A	B	C
1	2	**3**	4	**5**	6	7	8

ROOT

This  is the **C MAJOR TRIAD.**

DIRECTIONS: ❶ Circle the 1st, 3rd and 5th NOTES of each MAJOR SCALE. ❷ Create a MAJOR TRIAD on the STAFF to the right using the circled NOTES. ***The ROOT of each MAJOR TRIAD is given.***

SCALE of C MAJOR

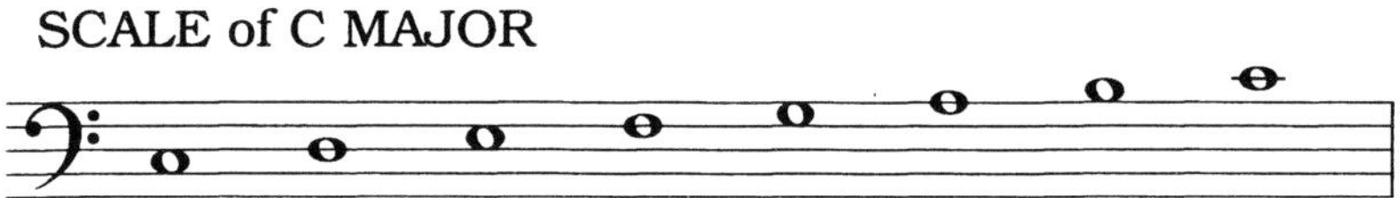

C	D	E	F	G	A	B	C
1	*2*	*3*	*4*	*5*	*6*	*7*	*8*

C MAJOR TRIAD

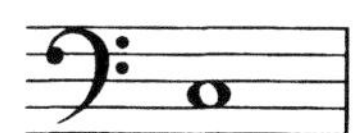

SCALE of F MAJOR

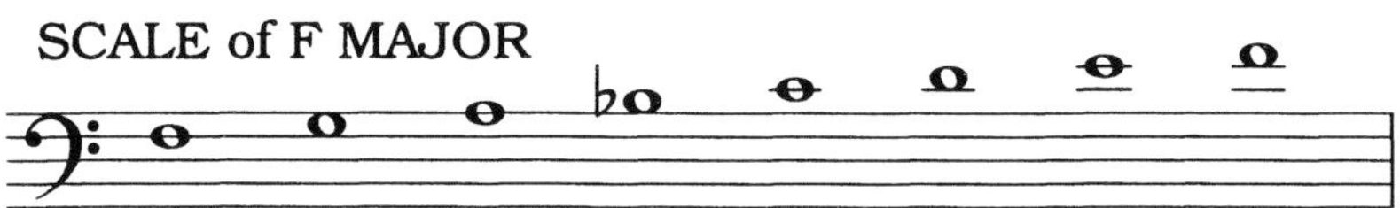

F	G	A	B♭	C	D	E	F
1	*2*	*3*	*4*	*5*	*6*	*7*	*8*

F MAJOR TRIAD

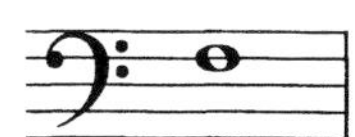

SCALE of G MAJOR

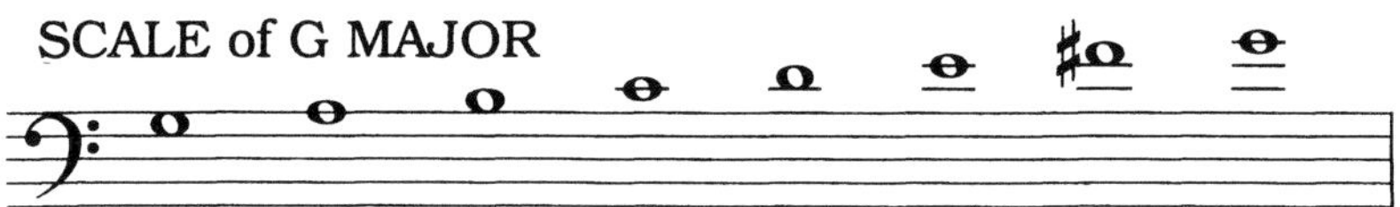

G	A	B	C	D	E	F♯	G
1	*2*	*3*	*4*	*5*	*6*	*7*	*8*

G MAJOR TRIAD

DIRECTIONS: Write the name of each MAJOR TRIAD on the dotted line.

LITTLE BROWN JUG

Moderato *U.S.*

TRIAD name → **C major** ....
Example

71. PRIMARY MAJOR TRIADS AND CHORD SYMBOLS

PRIMARY MAJOR TRIADS

TRIADS can be built on every NOTE of the MAJOR SCALE.

MAJOR TRIADS are found on the 1st (I), 4th (IV) and 5th (V) SCALE DEGREES.

ROMAN NUMERALS are used to represent CHORDS built on SCALE DEGREES.

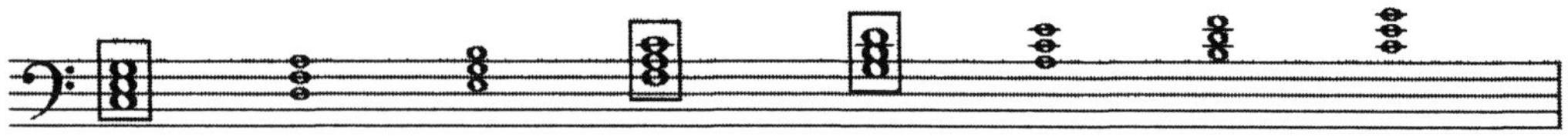

I C MAJOR — II — III — **IV** F MAJOR — **V** G MAJOR — VI — VII — **I** (8th DEGREE) C MAJOR

Many MELODIES can be HARMONIZED with the I, IV and V MAJOR TRIADS which are called the **PRIMARY MAJOR TRIADS**.

Below are the PRIMARY MAJOR TRIADS in the KEY of C MAJOR.

C MAJOR	*F MAJOR*	*G MAJOR*
I	IV	V

DIRECTIONS: Write the ROMAN NUMERAL and CHORD name for each MAJOR TRIAD.

COUNTRY GARDENS

Quickly *English*

ROMAN NUMERAL → I

CHORD name → **C MAJOR** ....

Example

These C Am D^7 are examples of CHORD SYMBOLS.

CHORD SYMBOLS represent various types of CHORDS.

Below are the PRIMARY TRIAD CHORD SYMBOLS for the KEY of C MAJOR.

C = 

F = 

G = 

***CHORD SYMBOL** for* **C MAJOR** — ***CHORD SYMBOL** for* **F MAJOR** — ***CHORD SYMBOL** for* **G MAJOR**

DIRECTIONS: ❶ Circle the CHORD SYMBOLS. ❷ Read each CHORD SYMBOL and then draw the proper MAJOR TRIAD on the BASS CLEF staff.

RED RIVER VALLEY

Moderately *U.S.*

Example

72. THE MINOR SCALE

This is the **C MAJOR SCALE.**

DEGREES: *1 2 3 4 5 6 7 8*

STEPS: 1 1 1/2 1 1 1 1/2

This is the **C MINOR SCALE.**

DEGREES: *1 2 3 4 5 6 7 8*

STEPS: 1 1/2 1 1 1/2 1 1

This **MINOR SCALE** (aka NATURAL MINOR) has HALF STEPS between the 2nd and 3rd, and the 5th and 6th DEGREES of the SCALE. All other STEPS are WHOLE STEPS.

Study how *OLD MACDONALD* has been changed from **C MAJOR** to **C MINOR.**

OLD MACDONALD in the **KEY of C MAJOR.**

OLD MACDONALD in the **KEY of C MINOR.**

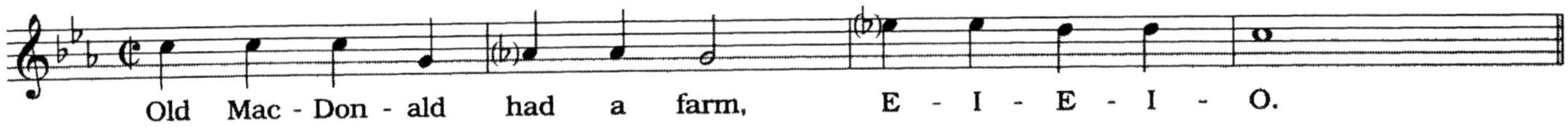

DIRECTIONS: Draw FLATS in the MELODY to change *CAMPTOWN RACES* from C MAJOR to C MINOR. ***Refer to the C MINOR SCALE NOTES at the top of this page.***

CAMPTOWN RACES

Study how HATIKVO is written in the **KEY of C MINOR.**

HATIKVO

Hebrew

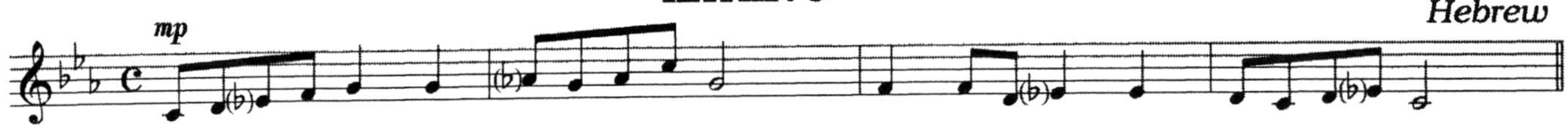

DIRECTIONS: Write *HATIKVO* in C MAJOR.

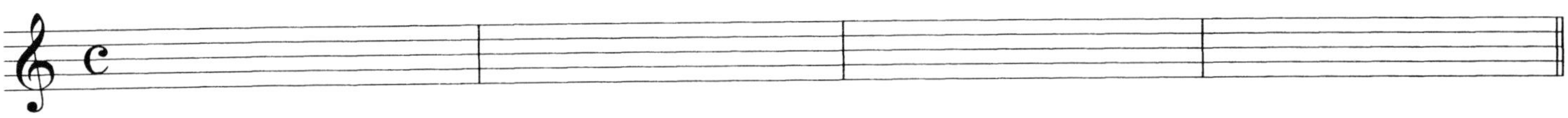

REVIEW OF LESSONS 69-72

DIRECTIONS: Write the chord style (block, broken or arpeggio) for *AMERICA* by Henry Carey.

Chord style → ....

DIRECTIONS: ❶ Circle the 1st, 3rd and 5th notes of each major scale. ❷ Create a major triad on the staff to the right using the circled notes. ***The root of each major triad is given.***

Scale of C Major

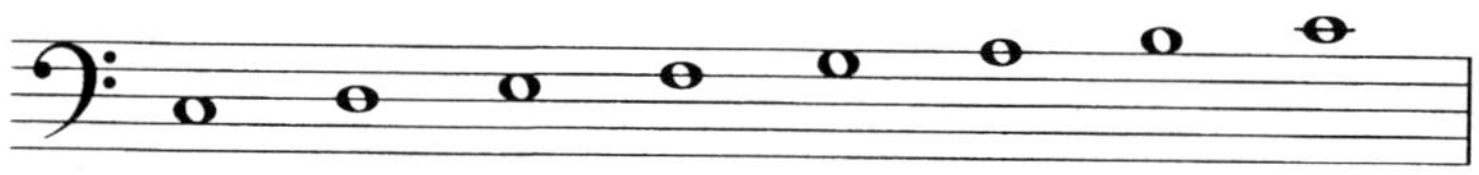

C D E F G A B C

C Major Triad

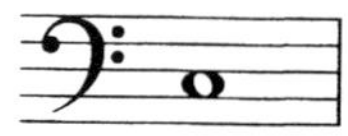

Scale of F Major

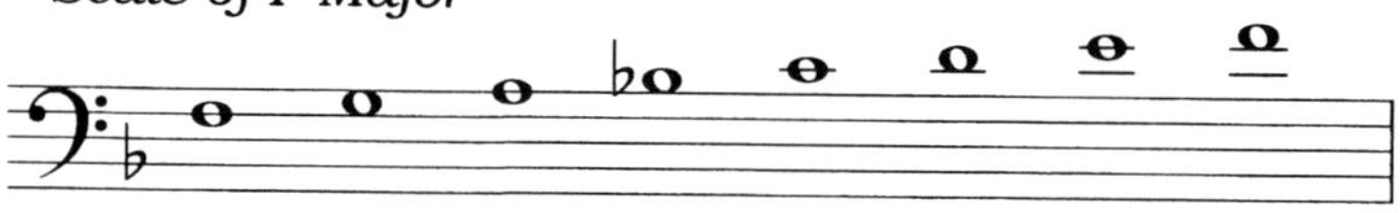

F G A B♭ C D E F

F Major Triad

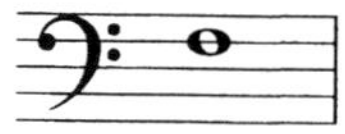

Scale of G Major

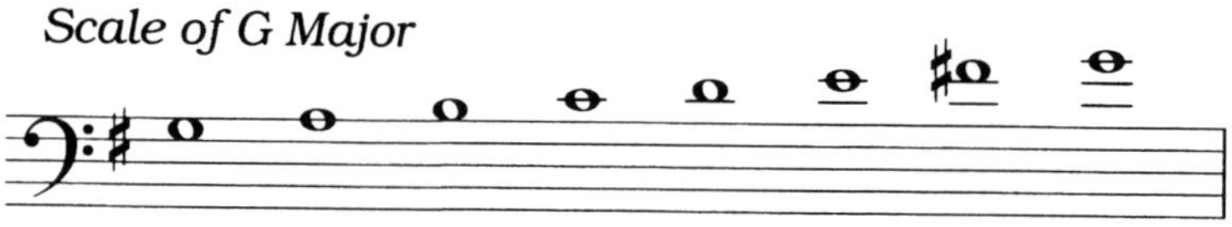

G A B C D E F♯ G

G Major Triad

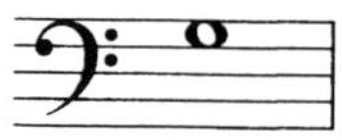

DIRECTIONS: Draw flats in the melody to change *TWINKLE, TWINKLE* from C major to C minor. ***Use the scales below for reference.***

C MAJOR SCALE

C MINOR SCALE

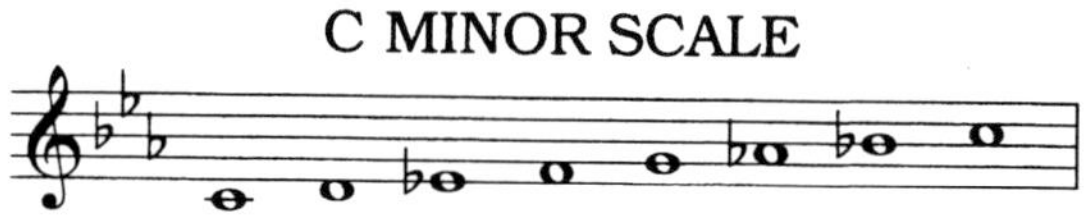

TWINKLE, TWINKLE LITTLE STAR

French

DIRECTIONS: ❶ Determine the key of *MY WILD IRISH ROSE* and then write the chord Roman numerals and chord names below the grand staff. ❷ Write the chord symbols in the boxes above the grand staff.

Roman numeral → **I**

Chord name → **C MAJ** ....

Example